B-26 MARAUDER
vs
Me 262

Europe 1945

ROBERT FORSYTH

OSPREY PUBLISHING

Bloomsbury Publishing Plc

Kemp House, Chawley Park, Cumnor Hill, Oxford, OX2 9PH, UK

29 Earlsfort Terrace, Dublin 2, Ireland

1385 Broadway, 5th Floor, New York, NY 10018, USA

E-mail: info@ospreypublishing.com

OSPREY is a trademark of Osprey Publishing Ltd

First published in Great Britain in 2025

A catalogue record for this book is available from the British Library.

ISBN: PB 9781472862594; eBook 9781472862600; ePDF 9781472862624; XML 9781472862617

25 26 27 28 29 10 9 8 7 6 5 4 3 2 1

Edited by Tony Holmes

Cover artwork and battlescene by Gareth Hector

Three-views, cockpit views, Engaging the Enemy artwork and armament views by Jim Laurier

Map and tactical diagram by www.bounford.com

Index by Zoe Ross

Typeset by PDQ Digital Media Solutions, Bungay, UK

Printed by Repro India Ltd

To find out more about our authors and books visit www.ospreypublishing.com. Here you will find extracts, author interviews, details of forthcoming events, and the option to sign up for our newsletter.

Acknowledgments

I would like to thank Eddie J. Creek, Tony Holmes, Michael O'Leary, Leslie Lotina and the Lotina family, Mike Parker, Rudolf Schallmoser, Mike Smith of b26.com, and Ted Young for their kind assistance in the preparation of this book, either recently or in the distant past. It is with sadness and gratitude I must also thank the late Lorenz Rasse and Jerry Scutts. Back in the early 1990s, several veterans from both sides, this story kindly provided their recollections either in person or by telephone or by letter. Sadly, they have left us, but I would once again like to acknowledge their invaluable and important contributions, without which this book would not have been possible – Adolf Galland, Walter Krupinski, Eduard Schallmoser, Henry Dietz, Albert Linz, Ronnie Macklin, Maj Gen John O. Moench (ret.), William P. Morton, Jonny Quong, Robert M. Radlein, Don E. Sinclair, John W. Sorrelle, James L. Stalter, and Warren E. Young.

B-26 Marauder cover artwork

In the spring of 1945, MY GAL SAL was B-26B-45 Marauder 42-95771 serving with the 37th BS/17th BG operating as part of the combined American and French First Tactical Air Force (Provisional) from bases in southern France, from where it provided air support to the Franco-American Sixth Army Group. On April 26, 1945, a force of Marauders drawn from the US 42nd BW and the French 11e *Brigade de Bombardement* was detailed to bomb the Luftwaffe base at Lechfeld and targets in the Schrobenhausen area. The B-26s of the 17th BG were assigned Lechfeld. Piloted by Lt Carl Johansen, MY GAL SAL was a relatively "veteran" aircraft of the 37th BS, having joined the group at Villacidro, in Sardinia, in February of the previous year. It was typical of the aircraft operated by the 17th BG, which encountered the Me 262s of JV 44 on numerous occasions over southern Germany and Austria in the final months of the war. That day, an encounter with a formation of the Luftwaffe jets led by Generalleutnant Adolf Galland would prove to be highly perilous for Johansen and his crew, whose aircraft would return to base on one engine. It was subsequently declared a write-off. (Artwork by Gareth Hector)

Me 262 cover artwork

Very representative of JV 44's initial "core" of jet interceptors which operated from Munich-Riem against the USAAF's medium bombers over southern Germany and Austria in 1945, Me 262A-1a Wk-Nr 111745 "White 5" is known to have been flown operationally by Unteroffizieren Eduard Schallmoser and Karl-Heinz Müller. The unit's usual tactics were to fly in *Ketten* of three aircraft. Installation of underwing batteries of 55mm R4M rockets was carried out depending on availability of both launch racks and rockets. These aircraft were devoid of any markings other than their national and tactical insignia. (Artwork by Gareth Hector)

Previous Page

Pilots of JV 44, clad in all-leather flight suits, walk from their Me 262s at Munich-Riem following the completion of a mission in April 1945. The tall figure at right is Unteroffizier Eduard Schallmoser, a recently qualified instructor pilot who engaged B-26 Marauder formations on several occasions. He claimed at least one Martin bomber shot down, but was hampered by problems with his equipment and armament on more than one occasion. (Robert Forsyth collection)

Contents

INTRODUCTION

After emerging in its initial form from the Glenn L. Martin plant in Baltimore, Maryland, in late 1940, the B-26 Marauder twin-engined medium bomber attracted some unfair criticism and in some quarters labored under a bad name. Among its detractors, it was felt that the aircraft's development had been rushed and, at best, it was considered to have been a "Respectable Floozie," while at worst, it became known alarmingly as the "Martin Murderer." According to an article published in *Time* magazine in January 1944:

> The B-26 was being called "The Flying Prostitute" (because some airmen thought that the 65ft wingspread, for so much airplane, constituted "no visible means of support"). By derivation, it became "The Baltimore Whore." Air Forces men gave it another sardonic tag, "The Widow-Maker." Student pilots started joking about it and ended up by scaring themselves. Training field crashes added to the legend of the ship's habits; she needed "all of Texas" for the takeoff; she came in to land like a cold flat-iron; she stalled like a Model T Ford running on kerosene. All that and much more.

Happily, however, the B-26 would prove its detractors wrong. The Marauder was an elegantly designed aircraft and, arguably, in terms of "looks" and proportion, it was ahead of any other medium bomber to see service in World War II. Its nearest rival in this regard was possibly the German Junkers Ju 88, against the performance of which, as a bomber, it compared well. The same applied pretty much to its home-based contemporary, the B-25 Mitchell. But unlike the Ju 88 and the B-25, which, in fairness, proved their adaptability as multi-role aircraft, throughout its wartime service, the B-26 remained a bomber – and a successful one at that. Powered by a pair of Pratt & Whitney R-2800 radial engines and flying, usually, with a crew of six, it could deliver a bombload of 2,000lb over a 500-mile radius.

The B-26 first went to war in the South Pacific in early 1942, where the 22nd Bombardment Group (BG) and two squadrons from the 38th BG operated the aircraft. Conditions in-theater were challenging. In its early months there, the 22nd BG operated from Port Moresby in New Guinea, which was described as a "malaria-infested hole" and where crews had to sleep under the wings of their aircraft using bedding and mosquito nets that had to be shipped in from Australia. To add to these discomforts, Port Moresby was the subject of several Japanese air attacks.

B-26s of the 17th BG cross the Italian coast following a bombing raid. The aircraft nearest the camera is 41-35183 of the 95th BS, an Omaha-built B-26C-25 — that plant's version of the Baltimore-built B-model. Coded "55," the aircraft seems not to have enjoyed a long operational career, as it was scrapped on July 2, 1943. Photo via Ronnie Macklin. (Robert Forsyth Collection)

Despite these local adversities, the unit carried out effective surprise low-level attacks in small formations of between two and six aircraft against enemy-held targets. These missions comprised 2,600-mile round trips, with a great part of them flown over shark-infested waters. The B-26s were even used as torpedo-bombers, and on June 13, 1942, with two torpedoes, they sank an Imperial Japanese Navy cruiser.

Furthermore, despite encountering enemy fighters, a small number of B-26 crews managed to chalk up aerial victories. On May 23, 1942, a lone Marauder bombed a target in Lae amidst torrential rain, dense anti-aircraft fire, and an attack by 15 A6M Zero-sen fighters. The crew claimed one shot down prior to returning to base. A few days later, on June 5, having bombed the same target, the crew of another B-26, flying on one engine, claimed four Zero-sens destroyed. After its first ten months of operations, the 22nd BG was credited with the destruction of 94 enemy aircraft. The Marauder had proved itself "respectable" and most definitely not a "floozie."

At around the same time Marauders were striking the Japanese in New Guinea, some 8,700 miles away, in Nazi Germany, engineers at the Messerschmitt aircraft company were in a jubilant mood, having brought a sleek new aircraft powered by a highly advanced and propellerless propulsion system to a state of flight-readiness. While not, strictly speaking, the world's first jet-powered aircraft to *fly*, the Messerschmitt Me 262 was to become the world's first military jet interceptor to fly *operationally*. This state-of-the-art fighter, with its shark-like fuselage and swept-back wings, first took to the air using pure jet power on July 18, 1942, when Messerschmitt test pilot Fritz Wendel made a trouble-free flight from Leipheim in the V3 (third prototype). The aircraft was fitted with a pair of Jumo 004A-0 (T1) turbojets. Despite the delayed gestation of both aircraft and powerplant, Wendel was able to report

Despite their aircraft not always enjoying the best of reputations, most combat-experienced Marauder crews became very proud of the B-26. Here, 2Lt Kenneth L. Bedor (standing, center) and his crew from the 37th BS/17th BG have gathered in front of their B-26F-1 42-96328 adorned with its self-explanatory nose art. Photo via Ronnie Macklin. (Robert Forsyth Collection)

generally smooth handling during the maiden test flight of the Me 262, achieving an unprecedented airspeed of 447mph.

German work on jet propulsion stretched back to the late 1930s, and by 1939 the Heinkel company had produced its diminutive He 178, essentially to test turbojet engines then under development by engineer Hans von Ohain. The He 178 V1 flew for the first time on August 27, 1939 fitted with a 500kp-thrust HeS 3b engine. In February of the following year, Ernst Heinkel's contemporary, Professor Willy Messerschmitt, had enhanced the design of his P.1065, a project which had been intended to fulfill a specification issued by the *Reichsluftfahrtministerium* (RLM) dating from January 1939 calling for a high-speed interceptor capable of a maximum speed of 560mph when powered by a single, unspecified jet engine.

Construction of the first P.1065 prototype, with a 35-degree swept-back wing, took place in February–March 1941, the project receiving the official RLM designation "Me 262" on April 8, by which stage the design had incorporated two Jumo (Junkers Motorenwerke) jet engines. Regardless of any misgivings Wendel may have harbored following his initial flight in July 1942, he noted that the Junkers engines "worked well."

The Me 262 was, indeed, a formidable and ground-breaking aircraft. As early as October 1943, the V3 was achieving test speeds of 590mph, whilst eight months later, the Me 262 S2 reached 623mph in a dive. In terms of offensive load, it was planned to install one 30mm MK 103 cannon and two 20 mm MG 151/20 cannon. There were low points, however, when some of the early prototypes crashed and two test pilots were killed.

Meanwhile, increased production of the B-26 Marauder had meant that the US Army Air Force (USAAF) was able to deploy two groups to the Twelfth Air Force in North Africa in November 1942, although initial operations did not go well. In emulating the low-level style of attack against German airfields, supply dumps, and ports as had been carried out in the Pacific, losses were suffered at the hands of enemy fighters and Flak. Operating conditions in Algeria also mirrored that of New Guinea, with crews sleeping in holes in the ground and eating in the open amidst heat, dust, and flies. The flightline of the 34th Bombardment Squadron (BS) was described as "nothing more than a barren clay expanse." The crucial issue, however, was that the B-26 units had been burdened with too many missions for just two bomb groups.

In 1943, a report was prepared on the performance of the B-26 in the Mediterranean Theater of Operations (MTO). Dismissing the tactical imbalance in force strength, it did not make for positive reading. This was on top of a spate of training accidents involving the Marauder in the US. On more than one occasion, committees were

convened to appraise the B-26 and, if necessary, to terminate further production of the aircraft, but, ultimately, this was never ordered. Indeed, in the spring of 1943 the first B-26 Marauders from the 322nd BG arrived in England for service with the Eighth Air Force, intended to form the nucleus of a new medium bomber wing. But without any firm tactical plan, the "low-level" doctrine was applied once more.

Meanwhile, in Germany, with RLM approval, Messerschmitt pressed ahead with further prototype production of the Me 262. In May 1943, the same month that 12 B-26s from the 322nd BG carried out the first low-level Marauder attack on a target in occupied Europe (a power station in the Dutch port of Ijmuiden), Generalmajor Adolf Galland, the commander of the Luftwaffe fighter arm, flew the Me 262 V4 from Lechfeld. Apparently brimming with enthusiasm, he informed Reichsmarschall Hermann Göring that, "It felt as if angels were pushing!"

Galland became a firm advocate for the further development of the jet interceptor, and wrote to his superiors that all measures should be taken to ensure swift mass production of the aircraft. In a report to the *Generalluftzeugmeister*, Generalfeldmarschall Erhard Milch, he stated:

> The aircraft represents a great step forward and could be our greatest chance; it could guarantee us an unimaginable lead over the enemy if he adheres to the piston engine. The flying qualities of the airframe make a very good impression. The engines are extremely convincing, except during take-off and landing. The aircraft opens up completely new tactical possibilities.

The path had been laid for what, in just under two years' time, would become an almost "private air war" fought over southern Germany between Galland's own unit of Me 262s and a small number of B-26 groups.

CHRONOLOGY

1886
January 17   Glenn L. Martin born in Macksburg, Iowa.

1898
June 26   Willy Messerschmitt born in Frankfurt am Main.

1911
October 19   Peyton M. Magruder, Chief Designer of the B-26, born in Fort Riley, Kansas.

The man behind the B-26 Marauder, Glenn L. Martin, photographed in May 1939. Martin combined the attributes of being a fervent devotee of aeronautics with a sharp and ambitious mind for business. By the time this photograph was taken in early 1939, design work on Model 179 had almost been completed. (Harris & Ewing collection, LOC, 2016875704)

1927
September 8   Willy Messerschmitt joins the Bayerische Flugzeugwerke at Augsburg, taking over project development.

1939
January   The US Army Air Corps (USAAC) issues Circular Proposal 39-640 for a twin-engined bomber. The Glenn L. Martin Company of Middle River, Maryland, proposes its design, with the company designation Model 179. Peyton M. Magruder is Project Engineer.

June   Design of Model 179 completed.

July 5   Model 179 submitted to Wright Field Board and accepted.

August 10   The USAAC issues a contract for 201 Model 179s under the designation "B-26."

December   Work commences on the Jumo T1 (004 A), forerunner of the Jumo 004 turbojet engine, at the Otto Mader Werke in Dessau.

1940
September 25   Maiden flight of the B-26, performed by Martin test pilot and Chief Engineer William K. Ebel, co-pilot Ed Fenimore and flight engineer Al Malewski.

November   First B-26 rolls off production line at Middle River.

1941
February 22   First four B-26s accepted by the USAAC.

1942

July 18   Messerschmitt test pilot, Fritz Wendel, makes the first turbojet-powered flight in the Me 262 V3 (third prototype) at Leipheim.

1943

May 1943   Generalmajor Adolf Galland test flies the Me 262 V4 at Lechfeld. He is impressed, and pushes for the Luftwaffe's quick utilization of the jet interceptor.

May 14   B-26s of the 322nd BG carry out the first Marauder bombing mission over Europe.

1944

April–July   First Me 262s reach the Luftwaffe with *Erprobungskommando* 262 at Lechfeld.

November   17th BG of the First Tactical Air Force moves to Rouvres-en-Plaines, France, from Corsica.

1945

January 23   Generalleutnant Adolf Galland, the Luftwaffe's commanding general of the *Jagdwaffe*, is formally dismissed by Reichsmarschall Göring.

February 9   323rd BG of the Ninth Air Force moves from Laon/Athies to Denain/Prouvy.

February 23   Me 262-equipped *Jagdverband* (JV) 44, commanded by Generalleutnant Galland, is established officially at Brandenburg-Briest.

March 31   JV 44 moves to Munich-Riem to commence operations.

April 5   344th BG moves from Cormeilles-en-Vexin to Florennes/Juzaine.

April 28   Galland orders transfer of JV 44 from Riem to Salzburg-Maxglan.

The designer of the Me 262, Professor Willy Messerschmitt (right) with one of his senior test pilots, Fritz Wendel. Despite Messerschmitt's almost obsessive enthusiasm for the Me 262, following extensive tours around the initial Luftwaffe operational units, Wendel tended to be less impressed with the jet's operational capability. (EN Archive)

DESIGN AND DEVELOPMENT

B-26 MARAUDER

In late January 1939, a document from the USAAC's Materiel Division landed on the desk of the successful 53-year-old aircraft designer and businessman Glenn Luther Martin at his factory in Middle River, Maryland, a few miles to the east of Baltimore on the Chesapeake Bay. Middle River was an unremarkable town, although it had seen considerable expansion during the 1930s as a result of an influx of Appalachian migrant workers. Indeed, Middle River owed much of its recent development to Glenn L. Martin, who had brought his eponymously named company to the town, where he had purchased 1,260 acres, from Cleveland, Ohio, 11 years earlier following an inducement offered by the Industrial Bureau.

A native of Iowa, Martin had led a varied and enterprising life and had enjoyed a fruitful career. At the age of two his family moved to the city of Liberal, Kansas, where his father ran a wheat farm and hardware store. Glenn demonstrated an early interest in aviation when, at the age of six, he built box kites on the kitchen floor that he subsequently sold for 25 cents apiece. The family moved to California in the early 1900s, and in late 1909, Glenn happily attended the first aviation meet at Dominguez Field near Los Angeles. His aeronautical interests never left him, and he went on to become the youngest manufacturer of aircraft in the world.

In 1909, at the age of 23, Martin learned to fly in a motorized biplane of his own design and build based on the Curtiss pusher-type, after which, despite being airborne for just 100ft at an altitude of two feet, he became known locally by the moniker "The Flying Dude." By this time, Martin had also built his own workshop in an abandoned church in Santa Ana, California, from where he built military trainers. Three years later, on May 10, 1912, he set the world record for over-water flight (some 76 miles) when he flew from Newport Bay, California, to Catalina Island, delivering, for the first time, mail on his way back.

In 1916, Martin entered into a brief partnership with the Wright Company, but the relationship was never good and a year later he reformed his own Glenn L. Martin Company based in Cleveland. In January 1918, he established a small factory in that city where, amongst other things, he worked on the design of a bomber, but this project never progressed. A keen publicist, Martin also claimed to be the first aviator to take his mother into the air; the first to film motion pictures from an aircraft; the first to deliver newspapers by air; the first to drop a baseball into a catcher's mitt from an aircraft; and, apparently, the first to hunt coyotes and escaped convicts by aircraft. He is also said to have picked up a passenger from a boat and to have searched the ocean for lost aviators, as well as being the first pilot to shower the public from the air with department store advertising and merchandise coupons. Martin would also teach William Boeing how to fly, subsequently selling him his first aircraft.

Martin went on to develop and build many different types for the USAAC and the US Navy during the 1920s, including the first night mail carriers, the first all-metal seaplane, and being the first pilot practical dive-bomber. By the late 1930s, the Glenn L. Martin Company was employing several thousand workers.

And so it was that the man who read the specification document for a twin-engined medium bomber issued by the USAAC in January 1939 did so with experience and a degree of confidence. Mindful of the clouds of war gathering over Europe, the USAAC had embarked upon an expansion program which included a need for a "300mph bomber" – i.e., one that could equal pursuit (fighter) speed. Circular Proposal 39-640 required a design for a twin-engined bomber with a speed of between 250–350mph, a range of 3,000 miles, a service ceiling of 20,000–30,000ft, and a crew of five. It was to carry a maximum bomb load of 4,000lb, with defensive armament provided by four 0.30-cal. machine guns.

This B-26-MA Marauder, assigned the USAAC serial number 40-1361, was photographed at the Martin Middle River plant in Maryland on November 25, 1940. The first production aircraft, it was airborne that same day for its maiden flight with William K. Ebel at the controls. (72004, RG18WP, NARA)

There was a tight deadline. Submissions would be opened on July 3, but Martin was not overly concerned that the Circular Proposal of January 23 had also been sent to seven other aircraft companies including Douglas, Stearman, and North American. The tendering process could be seen as daunting. Under what the USAAC called a "Method of Evaluation," design submission would be rated based on numerical grades awarded to each of the proposed aircrafts' most important characteristics. It was made clear that speed was the crucial factor.

Martin assigned the medium bomber project the company designation "Model 179" and delegated the task of designing it to 28-year-old engineer Peyton M. Magruder. The son of a brigadier general, Magruder had lived a peripatetic childhood, including periods in Manila, Yokohama, and Hawaii. Tall and with a keenness for sports, he won a place at the Naval Academy in Annapolis but left in 1934 and studied aeronautical engineering at the University of Alabama. Before completing his studies, however, Magruder found employment with the Naval Aircraft Factory in Philadelphia, but after two years, in 1937, he joined the Glenn L. Martin Company at Middle River as a project engineer.

Magruder and his small team rose swiftly and diligently to their assignment. They decided on a semi-monocoque, low-drag fuselage which was built in three sections and had four main longerons, transverse circular frames, and longitudinal stringers covered by aluminum skin. It had a circular cross section to which were attached shoulder-mounted wings.

Although the USAAC had not specified maximum landing or stall speeds, Magruder settled on a wingspan of just 65ft with a dihedral of only 1.3 degrees. This resulted in a wing loading in excess of 50lb per square foot. But this would be compensated for by a hydraulically actuated tricycle undercarriage. The nosewheel pivoted 90 degrees and retracted into the nose section while the main gear folded aft into the engine nacelles. Unusually, the wings had no fillets, but their relatively high position meant that the central fuselage could comfortably accommodate bombs, and there was plenty of ground clearance for what would be the aircraft's large propellers.

Early wind tunnel models comprised a twin vertical tail assembly to provide good aerodynamic control and handling, but this design was eventually replaced by a single fin and a fabric-covered rudder in order to give a maximum field of view from the required tail gunner's position. The tailplane was the first to feature a marked dihedral at eight degrees.

B-26C-45 MARAUDER

58ft 3in.

21ft 6in.

71ft 0in.

Model 179 was to be powered by two 1,850hp Pratt & Whitney R-2800-5 Double Wasp air-cooled radial engines, which were the most powerful available at the time. To maintain engine power up to medium altitudes, two-speed mechanical superchargers were installed, with engine exhaust being vented through ejectors on both sides of the closely cowled nacelles. The engines drove four-bladed Curtiss Electric propellers, 13ft 6in. in diameter, to which were fitted large, conical spinners with cuffs at the blade roots to enhance engine cooling. Model 179 (and what would eventually be the B-26) would be the first aircraft of World War II to use four-bladed propellers.

The two bomb-bays were arranged in tandem, with the doors to the forward bay folding in half along their length as they opened, while the rear bay doors opened in the more usual, simplified and standard way. Two 2,000lb bombs could be carried in the main, forward bomb-bay, or up to 4,800lb of smaller bombs if the aft bay was used as well.

Magruder and his team completed their work by late June 1939, and on July 5 Model 179 was submitted to the evaluation board of the Materiel Division at Wright Field. Glenn L. Martin had no qualms about what Magruder had produced, and it is alleged he exclaimed "This ship will win the competition!" upon examining the design drawings. Model 179 was indeed considered the best of the submissions, accumulating a rating of 813.6 points of a potential total of 1,000, with North American's competing NA-62 design proposal coming second with 673.4 points.

On August 10 the USAAC issued a contract to Martin for 201 aircraft under the designation "B-26," subject to approval. It was worth nearly $16,000,000. Approval was granted on September 10, with North American simultaneously winning a contract for its "NA-62" under which the company was to build 184 aircraft designated as the "B-25." On September 16 the order was confirmed for 139 B-26A models with self-sealing tanks and armor. Then, on September 28, a further order for 791 B-26Bs arrived – and this despite the fact that the B-model, which would feature a heightened rudder for greater stability, was still under design and not a single B-26 had yet flown.

For its part, Martin wasted little time and swiftly set up jigs at the Middle River plant. Mass production quickly followed, with the first B-26 rolling off the assembly lines soon enough to make its maiden flight on November 25 1940. The aircraft, Martin serial number 1226 (USAAF serial number 40-1361), was flown by the company's chief engineer and test pilot William K. "Ken" Ebel, with Ed Fenimore as co-pilot and Al Malewski as flight engineer. The flight was satisfactory, with a top speed of 315mph being attained, thus meeting the USAAC's speed requirement. Service ceiling reached 25,000ft, but as a result of changes introduced by the USAAC

Natural-metal B-26C-45 42-107614 leads camouflaged B-26C-25 41-35253 on a mission from France to a target in Germany in the fall of 1944. Both aircraft were assigned to the 323rd BG's 454th BS. Although the Marauder in the foreground would be lost to Flak damage at the end of its 12th combat mission on December 23, 1944, 41-35253 survived through to war's end. By then the veteran bomber had completed 96 combat missions. (USAF)

range dropped to 1,000 miles at 265mph with 3,000lb of bombs. Nevertheless, a further 113 hours of flight testing went well. Few modifications were required, although a slight overbalance to the rudder necessitated reversal to the rudder trim tab in the direction of travel.

Within four months the first four B-26s were delivered to the USAAC. They were accepted officially on February 22, 1941 and assigned to the 22nd BG (Medium) at Langley Field, Virginia. The group, which had previously operated B-18 Bolos, experienced some failures to nose gear struts which briefly delayed transition to full operational status. Although the struts were strengthened, the underlying problem was improper weight distribution – the first B-26s were delivered without guns, which meant that they had to be longitudinally trimmed using tools and spare parts for ballast. When the USAAC received the aircraft, they removed the ballast, thereby shifting the center of gravity forward and increasing loads on the nose gear. Installation of the guns corrected the problem.

In principle, there was cause for cautious encouragement, but problems such as the nose gear failure highlighted that what had been missed was the customary and vital elementary process of the in-depth testing of a dedicated prototype aircraft, or series of prototypes, with which to identify defects and shortcomings, and to eliminate them. Time had not allowed it. Regardless, the production effort at Martin went into full swing. It had to, for the situation in Western Europe had become extremely alarming. German forces had occupied France, the Low Countries, Denmark and Norway, and the war against Great Britain showed little sign of abating.

The Glenn L. Martin Company hired and trained thousands of new workers. In early September 1939 factory floorspace was expanded significantly, meaning the construction of new buildings at Middle River – all funded by the company. This was necessary as the plant was already turning out the Model 187, or Baltimore bomber, for the Royal Air Force (RAF), and it would also need space for output of the twin-engined PBM Mariner patrol bomber/flying boat for the US Navy. To assist workflow on the B-26, the company introduced several clever initiatives, including a "Robot Draftsman" – essentially a "photographic reproduction system" which could reproduce original drawings onto coated metal, wood, cloth, paper, and other materials, thus freeing up engineers to focus on more pressing and important tasks.

Aside from the B-26, the Glenn L. Martin Company designed and built the M-130 *China Clipper* and its famous sister seaplanes which flew Pan American's transpacific route from San Francisco to Manila, and the JRM Mars series of large, four-engined flying boat transports.

This well-weathered B-26 is typical of the Marauders that participated in the war in Europe. B-26F-1 42-96256 *UGLY DUCKLING* of the 454th BS/323rd BG was built at Middle River in 1944 and incorporated modifications to wings and equipment. It is seen here parked on pierced steel planking and covered in a protective tarpaulin at the 323rd BG's base at Denain-Prouvy, in France. The aircraft would be written off after being badly shot up by Me 262s from JV 44 over southern Germany just weeks after this photograph was taken. (Robert Forsyth Collection)

The company also constructed 531 B-29 Superfortresses and 1,585 B-26 Marauders at its other plant at Offutt Field, Omaha.

Me 262

With the ongoing development of the Me 262, Germany possessed the technology it needed to respond to the ever-growing threat of Allied air power in the West. It was not just Generalmajor Adolf Galland who believed this to be the case. On April 17, 1943, Hauptmann Wolfgang Späte, a Knight's Cross-holder and then 72-victory fighter ace, had flown the Me 262 V2 and reported to Galland that:

> Flight characteristics are such that an experienced fighter pilot would be able to handle the aircraft. In particular, the increase in airspeed when compared to the fastest conventional fighter deserves attention. This is not expected to decrease markedly when armament and radio equipment have been fitted. Characteristically, jet engines will not only maintain this speed at altitude but increase it. The climbing speed of the Me 262 surpasses that of the Bf 109G by 5–6m/sec. The superior horizontal and climbing speeds will enable the aircraft to operate successfully against numerically superior enemy fighters. The extremely heavy armament (six 30mm guns) permits attacks on bombers at high approach speeds with destructive results, despite the short time the aircraft is in the firing position.

Galland became a firm advocate for the further development of the jet, and wrote to his superiors that all measures should be taken to ensure swift and large-scale production of the aircraft. He also pushed for the immediate cancelation of the Me 209, the intended replacement for the Bf 109, so as to allow production of at least 100 Me 262s by the end of 1943. The enthusiasm he expressed to Generalfeldmarschall Erhard Milch, as mentioned in the Introduction to this book, may have been a little premature, for shortly afterwards, the director of testing at Messerschmitt, *Dipl.-Ing.* Gerhard Caroli, offered his own, more realistic appraisal of the Me 262 in which he warned, amongst other things, of problematical ailerons, high forces on the elevators and rudders, inadequate directional stability, poor stall behavior, and insufficient fuel injection.

But despite Professor Messerschmitt's misgivings over the cancelation of the Me 209, Galland won Milch's support and immediate priority was given to an initial Me 262 building program. It was to be plagued from the start. Firstly, production of the Me 209 was reinstated as a result of Messerschmitt complaining directly to Hitler, and thus emphasis was diverted from the Me 262 project. Secondly, a USAAF air raid on the Regensburg assembly plant in August 1943 destroyed crucial fuselage jigs and acceptance gauges and forced the company to relocate its project office from Augsburg to Oberammergau in the Bavarian Alps. Thirdly, a promise of 1,800 skilled workers needed to tool-up two production lines proved fickle, and they arrived late, resulting in the loss of almost three million man hours in nine months.

On November 2, 1943, Göring, accompanied by Milch, visited the bomb-damaged Regensburg works and met Messerschmitt. It was at this meeting that a new, previously unforeseen dimension crept in – the demands of Hitler. Göring enquired of Messerschmitt whether the Me 262 could carry bombs externally. "*Herr Reichsmarschall*," Messerschmitt replied, "It was intended from the beginning that the machine could be fitted with two bomb racks so that it could drop bombs, either one 500kg or two 250kg. But it can also carry one 1,000kg or two 500kg bombs." Göring was elated, replying, "That answers the *Führer*'s question."

Three days later, however, Göring and Milch were at Dessau, where they met Dr. Anselm Franz of the Junkers engine company. Bombs or no bombs, an aircraft cannot fly without engines. The design of the Me 262 incorporated a pair of Jumo 004 turbojet engines mounted beneath the wings, each unit comprising an eight-stage axial flow compressor, six separate combustion chambers, and a single-stage turbine.

The first production engines were delivered in May 1943, having been improved by modifications to the compressor and the turbine entry nozzles, which increased static thrust from 840kg to 900kg. Two months later, however, it was noticed that there were still "inconsistencies" in engine performance, with the Jumo 004 on the V3 and V4 prototypes suffering from burning after shutdown. The summer was dogged by flame-outs and leaking and igniting fuel, and Franz warned Göring and Milch of difficulties still being experienced with individual components including the turbine wheel, which suffered from vibration, and the control system, where there was

On April 17, 1943, Me 262 V2 Wk-Nr 262 000 0002 "PC+UB," distinctive here because of the absence of the type's later nosewheel, was assessed in flight by Major Wolfgang Späte, a 72-victory recipient of the Knight's Cross. He subsequently reported that, in his view, with its combination of high performance and heavy armament, the jet fighter would be able to prove effective against both enemy fighters and bombers. (EN Archive)

Me 262A-1a

34ft 7in.

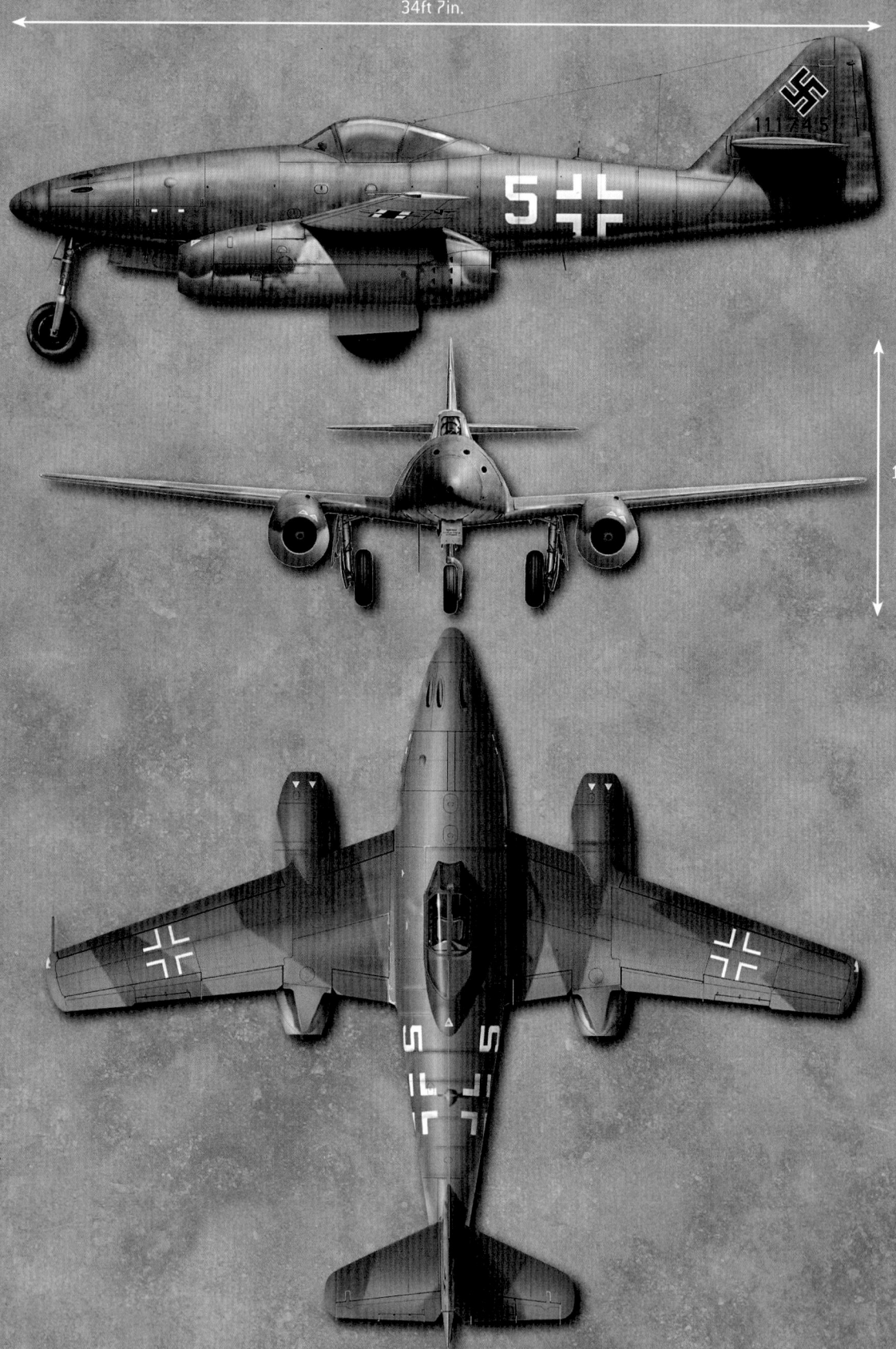

12ft 7in.

41ft 2in.

difficulty in opening and closing the throttles. "It cannot be guaranteed with certainty," Franz admitted, "That we will have the problem at upper altitudes rectified by the time series production begins so that the pilot will be able to open and close the throttles without worrying about a flame-out."

Göring seems to have been unworried by this, for on November 26 he invited Hitler to Insterburg, in East Prussia, in order that he could view a display of some of the Luftwaffe's latest aircraft and weaponry. Examples of the Me 163 rocket fighter were shown, as were new versions of the Ju 88 and the Arado Ar 234 jet bomber, the V1 flying bomb and new air-launched guided missiles. After a bungled commentary on the proceedings by Göring, the Me 262 V6 streaked past flown by Flugkapitän Gerd Lindner. Hitler was impressed. He asked whether the aircraft was able to carry bombs. Messerschmitt, also in attendance, eagerly stepped forward and again reiterated that the jet could carry a bombload of 1,000kg. Shortly afterwards Göring ordered the necessary trials to commence.

That Hitler asked if the Me 262 was able to carry bombs may have been a misguided question from a man who had little knowledge of air strategy and aircraft design, but, at the same time, it was perfectly understandable since every other frontline Luftwaffe combat aircraft had already proved itself adequately capable of carrying bombs or performing in the fighter-bomber role. What was different about the Me 262? Yet, six months later, in May 1944, on the Obersalzberg, Hitler had discovered from Milch that contrary to his orders that the Me 262 be produced exclusively as a fighter-*bomber*, the aircraft was, in fact, being built purely as a fighter. Hitler was exasperated and flew into a rage. Milch tried to reason with him, stating, "*Führer*, even the smallest child can see that this is a fighter and not a bomber."

Assisted by contacts in the RLM, the *Jägerstab* (Fighter Staff) and the armaments ministry, Galland managed to hold on to some degree of influence over the development program, steering the Me 262 towards deployment as a fighter. The aircraft eventually emerged as a twin-engined jet interceptor powered by two Jumo 004 turbojet units.

The first attempt at defining standardization came on May 8, 1943 when Messerschmitt engineers at Augsburg set out the planned production models, namely

OPPOSITE
Built at the Kuno AG *Werk* 1 at Scheppach (Burgau), Me 262A-1a Wk-Nr. 111745 was assigned the tactical number "White 5" by JV 44 and is known to have been flown by Unteroffizieren Eduard Schallmoser and Karl-Heinz Müller from Munich-Riem in April 1945. As one of the first batch of Me 262s used by the unit when it initially arrived at Riem, "White 5" was very representative of JV 44's core operational aircraft. The fuselage was finished predominantly in overall RLM 82 and featured only the "White 5" tactical number to distinguish it from other similarly camouflaged machines. The wing uppersurfaces were finished in a more strident RLM 82/83 splinter pattern. Its *Werk Nummer* was stenciled in black beneath the *Hakenkreuz*.

The familiar lines of the Me 262 emerge in the V5 prototype, "PC+UE." This was the first machine to be fitted with a nosewheel based on the piston-engined Me 309, an aircraft that never advanced beyond the experimental stage. The V5, which had a fixed undercarriage, flew for the first time on June 6, 1943. The landing gear's new "tricycle" arrangement provided improved forward vision for the pilot. Note the protective grilles fitted over the engine intakes. (EN Archive)

19

Eight new Me 262A-1as of the operational evaluation unit *Erprobungskommando* 262 lined up at Lechfeld in the summer of 1944. The aircraft in the foreground, Wk-Nr 170071 "White 2," was distinctive at the time of this photograph for having only two gun ports in its nose for 30mm MK 108 cannon, but four ammunition ejection chutes. Later, Me 262A-2a fighter-bomber variants would be fitted with only two cannon as standard. (EN Archive)

the A-1 fighter and the A-2 fighter-bomber. At this time, the Me 262, was still deep in its prototype testing phase, although it had been agreed that the A-model was to be an all-metal, single-seater with swept-back wings, powered by two turbojet units. In the standard A-1a fighter configuration, it was to be armed with four 30mm MK 108 cannon mounted in the nose.

If there was an Achilles' heel to development of the Me 262, it was engines – or rather the lack of them. As will be recounted, Professor Messerschmitt fought hard to try to get the RLM and the Junkers Motorenwerk to understand the urgency of the matter against a permanent background of shortages in materiel, parts, labor, and transport. It was therefore remarkable, in view of Allied bombing of the transport network, production centers, and airfields, and the ensuing production bottlenecks, that the Me 262A-1a, a fighter formed of entirely new concepts in aeronautical design and technology, reached the Luftwaffe so swiftly.

It now remained to be seen whether the aircraft would live up to expectations, and whether Galland's faith and optimism would be proved justified. For that, as Allied bombs began to rain down in ever greater numbers on the aircraft production plants and transport infrastructure, he would need an efficient supply chain, adequate numbers of aircraft, sufficient stocks of fuel and ammunition, and adequately trained pilots.

The shark-like fuselage and the adjustable *"Zwiebel"* ("onion") orifice cones of the Jumo 004B turbojets of the Me 262A-1a are seen to advantage in this photograph of Wk-Nr 111745 "White 5" of JV 44 at Munich-Riem in the spring of 1945. This aircraft is known to have been flown by several of the unit's pilots, most of whom were former NCO instructors on piston-engined fighters who had hastily transitioned to flying the jet interceptor. (Robert Forsyth Collection)

TECHNICAL
SPECIFICATIONS

B-26 MARAUDER

From 1943, the B-26 appeared in four major variant series, all known by the general type name of "Marauder" – a name given to the aircraft by the RAF, which, in October 1941, had ordered 52 later production B-26As, operating them as the Marauder I.

The first B-26s to see combat with the USAAF in Europe were of the B-4 type, which introduced a longer nosewheel leg to give the aircraft a higher wing incidence to reduce its take-off run, four forward-firing fuselage package guns for use by the pilot, and provision for a pair of 0.50-cal. machine guns in the rear fuselage hatches. Produced at Middle River, the B-model can be considered the "main" variant, being built in several production blocks, each incorporating successive improvement. The first B-model came off the assembly line in May 1942 fitted with Pratt & Whitney R-2800-41 engines. These were two-row, 18-cylinder, air-cooled radial designs, displacing 2,804 cubic inches, with a bore of 5.75in. and a stroke of 6in. They produced 2,000hp at take-off and 1,600hp at 13,500ft.

Maximum speed at 14,500ft was 317mph, but weight increased to 28,000lb empty and 34,000lb fully loaded, including 3,000lb of bombs. The R-2800 also incorporated one of the most advanced baffle systems to control cooling air flow, and at the time of its introduction no other air-cooled engine and only a few inline

B-26 MARAUDER WAIST GUNS

The two 0.50-cal. Browning AN/M2 machine guns were gravity fed, with each weapon having a magazine containing 240 rounds. Sliding hatches covered the waist gun positions when they were not in use. Typically, the B-26 crew's radio operator would also man both waist guns, although a second crewman could help out if required. The waist gunners appear to have done the main bulk of firing and defense against the Me 262s as they swept through the Marauder formations in April 1945.

1. Machine gun ammunition magazines
2. Starboard gun ammunition feed belt
3. Port ammunition feed belt
4. Starboard gun door and window
5. Port gun door and window
6. Machine gun mounting plate and swivels
7. Ammunition feed belts for tail guns
8. Port 0.50-cal. Browning AN/M2 machine gun
9. Starboard 0.50-cal. Browning AN/M2 machine gun
10. Gunners' jump seats

water-cooled engines could match the R-2800's power-to-weight ratio. The engines drove Curtiss electric propellers, with the angle of the blades controlled while in flight to provide maximum efficiency and to maintain constant engine speed under varying operating conditions.

The B-1 saw the spinners removed, new engine cowlings with enlarged air intakes, additional armor, revised twin tail guns and a 28in. extension to the fuselage. Following a run of 641 B-1s to B-5s, all of which featured progressive minor improvements, the next main variant was the B-10. This became recognized as the "long-wing model," with its wingspan increased by six feet to 71ft in an attempt to reduce wing-loading. The aircraft was 58ft 3in. in length, 21ft 6in. in height, and had a wing area of 658sq ft. As the December 1944 manual stated:

> The B-26 has a high wing loading. It can take plenty of punishment, but you must know and respect its tolerances. It wasn't built for aerobatics, inverted flight, or violent stall maneuvers. It is not a pursuit-type airplane.

Armament comprised a maximum of 12 0.50-cal. Browning AN/M2 machine guns, including, in addition to the flexible nose gun used by the bombardier, a fixed gun in the starboard side of the nose section. Like the twin forward-firing package guns mounted on either side of the lower curve of the forward fuselage and intended for strafing, this weapon was fired from the pilot's control column. However, the fixed gun made the nose area crowded, and so was subsequently removed in the ensuing B-45.

A Martin 250CE electrically powered dorsal turret was located forward of the waist gun hatches and just aft of the rear bomb-bay. It was designed as a "drop-in" unit and was "hung" from the upper fuselage, rotating continuously in azimuth to elevate the two 0.50-cal. machine guns from five degrees below to 85 degrees above the horizontal. Ammunition was fed to the guns by two automatic electric booster motors from two 400-round boxes in the forward part of the turret. The profile of the aircraft was protected from gunfire by an interrupter which was interwired with the firing mechanism. Hand grips with built-in gun triggers controlled the turret's rotation and gun elevation. Also located on the grips were a microphone and a high-speed switch. Connections for heated flying suits, oxygen, and the interphone ran into the turret through a swivel fitting. Master switches for azimuth and elevation power were under the gunner's seat. A camera, gunsight rheostat, and gun safety switches were installed to the right of the seat.

A radio operator/gunner test fires his starboard 0.50-cal. manually operated weapon. The gunner operated both waist guns on either side of the fuselage, each of which were provided with 240 rounds. Later models saw the introduction of blast deflectors on the outside of the fuselage to help protect the gunner from the slipstream. (USAF)

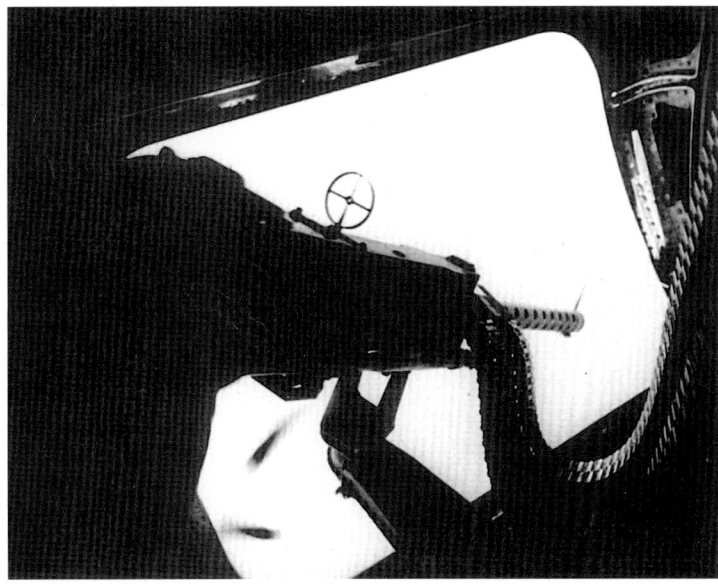

— The B-10 received mechanically improved R-2800-41 engines, although there was no increase in horsepower. The tail was increased in height and area to improve yaw stability.

The B-model series blocks ran through to the B-55. Again, interim blocks incorporated changes and/or refinements. The B-15 saw changes to the oxygen system and was the last variant to have the "stepped" tail gun position with its two hand-held weapons. The B-20 had further changes to the oxygen system, a shorter chord rudder and, starting with the B-26B-20 and B-26C-20, a Bell Type M-6 powered tail "stinger" with two 0.50-cal. machine guns along with armor plate for the gunner. The guns, fitted with G-11 solenoids, were mounted side-by-side.

The Bell Sundstrand system installed in the M-6, consisting of two hydraulic pumps and a motor in one unit, azimuth and elevation vanes, and a control unit mounted on the back of the armor plate, was designed to provide remote control of gun movement. Gun charging handles were installed in the most forward position on each gun, and they were accessible through the armor plate doors. The firing triggers were incorporated in the gun mount control grips. Aiming of the guns was undertaken using an N-8 illuminated sight mounted immediately forward of the window in the armor plating.

The B-26B-25 had its rear bomb-bay sealed to prevent overloading and the B-55 had an improved bombsight.

The B-26C, which appeared in mid-1942, covered all of the models produced at the Omaha plant through to the C-45, which saw the end of production in the spring of 1944. The F-series referred to the "twist-wing" model which had a seven-degree angle of incidence, appearing after the F-6. This wing modification was again intended to shorten the take-off run, although maximum speed was compromised. However, only the B-26F-1 was delivered to the USAAF.

The last production model, the B-26G, differed only slightly from the F. Aside from being powered by Pratt & Whitney R-2800-43 engines, the aim of the G-model was to incorporate standard equipment used by both the USAAF and US Navy wherever possible to aid in the interchangeability of parts. There were eight principal

B-26 MARAUDER TAIL TURRET

From the B-26B-20 and B-26C-20, the hand-held "Twin Fifty Stinger" tail gun assembly seen in previous models of the Marauder was replaced by a power-operated Bell Type M-6 turret again fitted with 0.50-cal. Browning AN/M2 machine guns. The M-6 had a transparent Plexiglas cap through which the guns protruded, the weapons being hydraulically-boosted to give a 90-degree cone of fire behind the aircraft. The gunner was protected by extensive armor plating installed between him and his weapons. The turret was operated by a Bell Sundstrand hydraulic pump system that moved the N-8 illuminated gunsight and the machine guns in tandem. The 0.50-cal. weapons could be rapidly moved at up to 35 degrees per second.

1. N-8 illuminated gunsight
2. Gun traverse and elevation controls
3. Gun firing buttons
4. Armored glass
5. Gunner's armor plating
6. Bell Sundstrand hydraulic pump system
7. 0.50-cal. ammunition feed belts
8. Gunner's seat

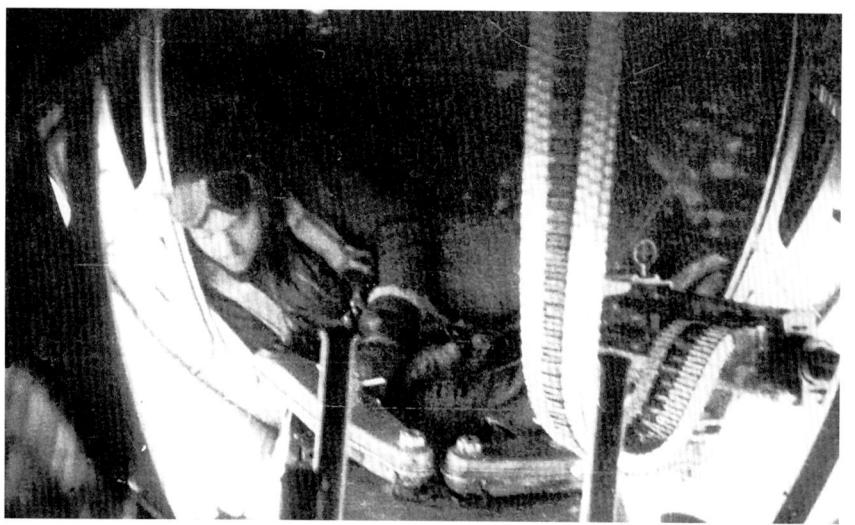

TSgt Robert M. Radlein, a radio operator/gunner with the 454th BS/323rd BG, peers down from the waist hatch of a B-26G during a mission over southern Germany on April 16, 1945. Four days later, Radlein fired at two Me 262s of JV 44 as they attacked a formation of Marauders from the 323rd BG over Memmingen. Photo via Robert M. Radlein. (Robert Forsyth Collection)

B-26G blocks (G-1, G-5, G-10, G-11, G-15, G-20, G-21, and G-25). Early examples were fitted with a "blast blanket" intended to protect the structure of the forward fuselage around the package guns, as well as modifications to the fuel and hydraulic lines and an emergency landing system. Other blocks had changes to the portable oxygen and radio systems.

The main fuel tanks in the B-, C-, and early F-models each held 360 gallons and were installed in the wings, inboard of the nacelles. The outboard auxiliary tanks each held 121 gallons. Fuel was supplied to the engines exclusively from the main tanks. In the later F- and G-models, the capacity increased to 380 gallons for the main tanks and a gallon less in the auxiliaries.

The hydraulics in the B-26 featured an open system of the accumulator-pressure regulator type, meaning that hydraulic fluid was supplied from the main hydraulic reservoir to two engine-driven pumps under atmospheric pressure.

The communication equipment in the F- and G-models comprised a ten-station interphone system, two medium-frequency and low-frequency command receivers, two medium-frequency command transmitters, a four-channel VHF command transmitter and receiver, an all-frequency (except VHF) liaison transmitter, a marker beacon receiver, an all-channel IFF transponder, an emergency transmitter, and a frequency meter. According to the pilot's manual, "The radio equipment which you have in the B-26 is the best that American ingenuity has been able to produce."

As previously mentioned, the rear bomb-bay was sealed and its bombing equipment removed. The forward bay had four vertical racks, with a total of 20 bomb stations. Each station had B-7 shackles and either A-2 or A-4 release units. Ordnance combinations consisted of two 2,000lb or 1,600lb demolition bombs, four 1,100lb demolition bombs, six 600lb demolition bombs, eight 300lb demolition bombs, or 20 100lb demolition bombs. The bomb-bay doors were opened hydraulically from the bombardier's compartment. Bombs could be released using an electric selective release or a bomb release intervalometer control set for either selective or train release, or a manual salvo release of all bombs simultaneously.

Emergency equipment included a six-man life raft stowed above the navigator's compartment, two crash axes and a Lux engine fire extinguisher installed in each nacelle, the controls for which were located on the floor between the pilot's and co-pilot's seats. There were also windshield defrosters, wing de-icers, a propeller anti-icing system, an Aldis signal lamp, and a Very pistol, the latter two items in the radio operator's compartment.

Me 262A-1a

The main day fighter variant of the Me 262 to see operational service was the A-1a.

The first attempt at defining standardization came on May 8, 1943 when Messerschmitt designers at Augsburg issued *Projektübergabe* ("Project Delivery") *IV*, "*Me 262 Jäger und Jabo*," which set out the planned production models, the A-1 fighter and the A-2 fighter-bomber. At this time, the Me 262 was still deep in its prototype testing phase, although it had been finalized that the A variant was to be an all-metal, single-seater with swept-back wings and powered by two turbojet units.

The *Projektübergabe* was followed on October 29, 1943 by *Protokoll Nr.19*, which described the A-1 in greater detail, confirming that it was to be a single-seat interceptor powered by a pair of Jumo 004B-1 jet engines. The aircraft was to be armed by four 30mm MK 108 cannon with a total of 360 rounds, a fuel load of 2,570 liters, and appropriate radio equipment for day fighter operations.

The problem was the availability of the engines. Fearful of the appearance of Allied jet aircraft later that year, Professor Messerschmitt wrote to the production director of the Jumo engine plant at Dessau on April 20, 1944 imploring him to overcome the problems – and thus delays – associated with delivery of the badly needed Jumo 004 engines. "It is a matter of life and death for us all to set up the numbers of Me 262s with your engines as rapidly as possible."

An excellent view of the port side Jumo 004 jet engine of Me 262A-1a Wk-Nr 500071 "White 3," flown by Fähnrich Hans-Guido Mütke of 9./JG 7, which force-landed in Switzerland on April 25, 1945. The Jumo 004, seen here with the aircraft rested on wooden blocks and jacks, represented the zenith of jet engine development at this time, and placed the Luftwaffe ahead of the Allies. (EN Archive)

Production was authorized, but actually building the Me 262 under the constant threat of Allied bombing was another matter. On April 25, the day after the Eighth Air Force had bombed the Messerschmitt assembly plant at Leipheim where the jet was being built, Dr. Heinz Krome, a member of the *Jägerstab*, told Generalfeldmarschall Milch, the chairman of an emergency production committee, that it was "a choice between the V2 [rocket] in a year or the Me 262 in three or four months." But Messerschmitt's personal efforts, and those of the members of the *Jägerstab* able to fully understand Germany's predicament and exert influence, somehow won through.

In its usual form, the Me 262A-1a was an elegant, low-wing, all-metal, twin-jet, single-seat interceptor with 18.5-degree sweptback wings bearing a span of 41.2ft, a shark-like fuselage 34.7ft in length incorporating a nosewheel, and a large, high tail assembly to which were fitted horizontal stabilizers also with sweptback leading edges. The equipped weight, allowing for a pilot, ammunition, and a fuel load of just over 1,800 liters, was 13,390lb.

The pilot was accommodated in a self-contained sub-assembly which held the instrument panel and electrical controls, stick and rudder, throttles, seat and battery. This "*Wanne*" ("tub") was designed to break free on impact in the case of a crash-landing, offering the pilot some degree of enclosed protection – a measure that, as will be recounted, would play an important part in the survival of one of the top aces serving with JV 44. The cockpit was capped by an all-round-vision, hinged canopy.

The instrument panel held a large number of gauges and dials but was well laid-out. The key flying gauges such as the airspeed indicator, altimeter, compass, turn and bank indicator, artificial horizon, and rate of climb indicator were located on a panel to the left, while engine controls, injection, gas pressure and temperature indicators were grouped to the right. An arm-level panel to the left of the pilot housed the undercarriage and oxygen controls, with the radio and electrics on a similar panel to the right. The Me 262A-1a was provided with a FuG 16ZY transmitter/receiver and a FuG 25a IFF set.

The two Junkers Jumo 004B-1 turbojet engines each comprised an eight-stage axial compressor with single-stage turbines producing 8.8kN of thrust at 8,700rpm. The B series engine saw improvements over the A series used on the early Me 262 prototypes. This included modified compressor construction using a rotor with separate discs, the replacement of castings with sheet metal where possible, improved entry to the air intake and the substitution of more than half the weight of strategic material used in the A-series engine (although solid turbine blades were still fitted). A Jumo 004 unit was 12.4ft long and weighed between 1,609–1,653lb. These ground-breaking, state-of-the-art engines gave the Me 262 a climbing speed of 33ft/sec at 19,685ft (seven minutes) and 17ft/sec at 29,500ft (14 minutes). Maximum range at 19,685ft was 323 miles and 400+ miles at 29,500ft.

Standard fuel tankage totaled 2,570 liters of J2 fuel contained in four internal tanks, with provision for two ETC 503 external racks each holding a 300-liter drop tank. J2 was a brown, low-grade, coal oil fuel similar to diesel oil, and was usually available in ready supply in 1944 despite transport problems.

In the standard fighter/interceptor configuration, the Me 262 was armed with four 30mm MK 108 cannon mounted in the nose. Manufactured by Rheinmetall-Borsig, the MK 108 was a blow-back operated, rear-seared, belt-fed cannon, using

Me 262A-1a MK 108 CANNON

The standard installation of four 30mm belt-fed, electrically-ignited Rheinmetall-Borsig MK 108 cannon in the nose of an Me 262A-1a interceptor of JV 44. When used at close range in the hands of a skilled pilot, the effect of such armament against enemy bombers could be devastating. However, although a powerful weapon, the MK 108's cheapness and its ease of manufacture using pressed metal stampings made it prone to jamming and other forms of malfunction. The cannon's slow rate of fire also reduced its effectiveness when used in combat by the high-speed Me 262. Note the proximity of the nosewheel housing to the gun bay, as well as the electric ignition cable at the rear of the cannon installation and the spent ammunition discharge chutes.

electric ignition, being charged and triggered by compressed air. The prime benefit of this weapon, used profusely by the Luftwaffe for close-range, anti-bomber work from early 1942 onwards, lay in its simplicity and economic process of manufacture, the greater part of its components consisting of pressed sheet metal stampings.

With the advent of massed American daylight bomber formations bristling with concentrated defensive firepower, the need arose for a long-range, heavy caliber gun with which a German pilot could target specific bombers, expend the least amount of ammunition, score a kill in the shortest possible time, and yet stay beyond the

range of the defensive guns. It was a virtually impossible requirement, and yet the MK 108 almost achieved this when used by later variants of the Bf 109 and the Fw 190A-8, where it quickly earned a fearsome reputation amongst Allied bomber crews. Two types of shells could be loaded, the 30mm high-explosive tracer type "M" shell designed to cause blast effect and the 30mm high-explosive incendiary shell.

Generalmajor Adolf Galland recalled the gun being installed in the Me 262s of his unit, JV 44:

The Revi (*Reflexvisier*) 16b gunsight was a standard fitting in the Me 262A-1a. Here, it is seen lowered and locked away to the right of the instrument panel. The gunsight was raised for its combat setting and the reflector glass panel pulled up. It incorporated a sun visor, night vision filter, light bulb, and dimmer switch. Just below the gunsight in this photograph at the top of the instrument panel are, from left to right, the variometer and two tachometers. (EN Archive)

Firstly, it was, constructionally speaking, extraordinarily easy to install four MK 108s into the aircraft. Secondly, it was good to have a gun which solved all our problems; that is to say a gun which had a rapid rate of fire and great destructive effect, although there was the disadvantage of an insufficiently flat trajectory. There were snags. The guns were not that much good when you were banking because the centrifugal forces arising from such a maneuver ripped the belts holding the shells. But these teething troubles were easily sorted out by a well-trained ground crew.

Initially, it was foreseen that a Revi (*Reflexvisier*) 16b reflector gunsight would be installed, a tried and tested type used by the Luftwaffe's fighter units for much of the war. It was also planned to fit as many Me 262s as possible with the new EZ 42 gyroscopic sight, which would allow a pilot to fire at a target without allowance for the movement from fixed guns built into the longitudinal axis of the carrying aircraft. When approaching a target, the pilot had to ensure that he continuously twisted the range-finding button on the aircraft's control column so that the growing target was permanently encapsulated in the dial, as well as making sure that the crosswire was contained within the aiming circle on the target. The precise angle of deflection was obtained within two seconds. Accuracy could be guaranteed to within 15 percent of the angle of deflection in the longitudinal direction of the enemy and ten percent perpendicularly.

Despite lacking numbers, the appearance of the Me 262 gave those Luftwaffe pilots slated to fly the jet cause for both encouragement and trepidation. Encouragement, because finally they had an aircraft with which they could power past and away from most Allied escort fighters to get to the bombers, but trepidation as a result of having to learn and master an entirely new form of propulsion capable of unprecedented speed and to turn the aircraft into an efficient tactical asset.

THE STRATEGIC SITUATION

The essence of this book focuses on the actions fought between a number of USAAF B-26 medium bomber groups and the Me 262 interceptors of the Luftwaffe's JV 44 over southern Germany from early April 1945 to the end of the war. As such, in terms of the wider European air war, the sphere and degree of operational activity were relatively limited, despite such activity being of an extremely intensive nature. This being said, to place the activity in context, it is necessary to understand what brought both sides to the point of engagement.

From mid-1943, the Allied strategic air offensive against Nazi Germany intensified in scope, range, force strength, and destructiveness. From then, and for nearly two years, almost night-by-night and day-by-day, RAF Bomber Command and the USAAF systematically pulverized Germany's cities and production centers, bombed its refineries, paralyzed its transport system, attacked its airfields, terrorized and killed its civilians, and eventually went a long way to obliterating its armies as they defended what remained of their territory.

History and historians have tended to focus their attention on the meritorious operations of the "heavy" bomber units of the USAAF's Eighth Air Force and RAF Bomber Command against targets in Germany and occupied Europe. That is to say the B-17 Flying Fortresses and B-24 Liberators flown by the Americans, and the Lancasters and Halifaxes flown by British and Commonwealth crews. These aircraft and their units accomplished significant and war-winning results, albeit with heavy losses. But the destruction they wreaked upon the enemy in terms of both precision and area bombing, was only one element of the overall Allied 'strategic' bombing aim.

By day, operating in concert with the "*Viermots*" ("four-engines"), as the B-17s and B-24s had been christened by the Luftwaffe's fighter pilots, were squadrons of twin-engined medium bombers tasked with the role of conducting lower-level precision attacks in smaller formations against specific targets. As mentioned in the Introduction to this book, in the late spring of 1943 the Eighth Air Force had formed a new medium bomber wing, the 3rd Bombardment Wing (BW), in which the first British based B-26 units – the 322nd and 323rd BGs (the latter bringing 60 long-span C-6s to England) – were grouped.

However, the reality was that flying lower-altitude missions into enemy territory protected by a technologically advanced radar detection network which was linked to a dense "wall" of Flak guns on the ground and well-positioned fighters commanded by experienced unit leaders in the air was a highly dangerous and, ultimately, costly initiative. Flak was the main danger, however, and few Marauders would return to base from missions free of damage or without wounded crew. By mid-July 1943, this state of affairs was fully recognized, and the first two Marauder groups, as well as the B- and C-models of the 386th and 387th BGs, which had also arrived in England in June and July, underwent revised training for medium altitude missions. As soon as August, however, VIII Air Support Command settled on a policy of solely medium altitude bombing.

In October 1943, all four of the B-26 groups were transferred to the newly reactivated Ninth Air Force, which had been formed in the Western Desert in 1942 to undertake a "tactical" role. Subsequently moved to England, it was developed once again into a tactical force to support the Allied invasion of France. This was timely, for within a month of the Ninth's reactivation, Allied air intelligence, with the assistance of aerial reconnaissance and photo interpretation, had identified German V1 flying bomb launch sites (quickly dubbed "ski sites" on account of the control buildings resembling the shape of skis from the air) in France. These were difficult targets to hit using high-altitude "heavy" bombers, and so the "medium" tactical B-26 units (as well as RAF tactical bombers) were called upon to do the job in missions that were given the codename *Noball*. Thus, the four B-26 groups commenced an almost round-the-clock bombing offensive against the launch sites in November 1943.

Capt (later Maj Gen) John O. Moench was a B-26 pilot with the 323rd BG based at Earls Colne. He remembered:

The V1 sites were pretty damned well defended – but that depended on how you count and how black your sky became. A dozen 88mm guns was not unusual – sometimes a lot

English Channel

Dunkirk

Calais

Lille

Arras

BELGIUM

Brussels

Liège

Namur

② Denain-Prouvy

Florennes/Juzaine

Abbeville

Amiens

Compiègne

Cormeilles-en-Vexin

③

Reims

Verdun

Paris

FRANCE

Troyes

Orléans

Auxerre

1. **17th BG:** Rouvres-en-Plaine, France (Y-9), November
   1944–June 1945 (to Hörsching, Austria [R-87])
2. **323rd BG:** Denain-Prouvy, France (A-83),
   February–May 1945 (to Gablingen, Germany [R-77])
3. **344th BG:** Cormeilles-en-Vexin, France (A-59),
   October 1944–April 1945, then to Florennes/Juzaine
   (A-78) April–September 1945 (to Schleissheim,
   Germany [R-75])

N

0   25 miles

0   25km

Dijon

① Rouvres-en-Plaine

B-26B-20 41-31951 *USO/ Thunderbird*, a "white tail" of the 454th BS/323rd BG, forms a backdrop to an almost peaceful scene at either Earls Colne, in Essex, or an airfield in France after the Allied landings. Pre- and post-*Overlord*, the Marauders of the Ninth Air Force carried out an intensive and effective bombing campaign against V-weapon sites, railways and repair workshops, naval facilities, and ammunition and fuel depots. Photo via Jerry Scutts. (Robert Fosyth Collection)

more. They were not like the later Ruhr numbers we had to fly, but often the sites were located in proximity to some heavily defended targets, the fire from which could not be avoided going in or coming out.

The raids continued throughout the first two months of 1944, almost on a daily basis, but to the launch sites were added enemy airfields, storage facilities, and transport targets. It was quite usual for the Marauders to fly multiple sorties in one day from their bases in Essex. It was draining work. Sometimes, this was on account of the limited bombloads carried by B-26s, which necessitated repeat visits to targets. One B-26 of the 322nd BG notched up its 50th mission in January 1944.

By late February 1944, the Ninth Air Force's IX Bomber Command numbered three Combat Bombardment Wings (M) comprising one A-20 Havoc "light" bomb group and six B-26 Marauder "medium" bomb groups.

In the lead-up to the Normandy landings, the B-26 units maintained their pace of operations, although target priorities changed depending to a great extent on what the "heavies" of the Eighth Air Force were doing. From March 1944, as support for the strategic air offensive, the priority order for the medium bombers was Luftwaffe airfields followed by marshaling yards, E-boat and R-boat pens, railway repair workshops, and *Noball* sites. Such was the importance of this tactical "support" bombing that by the end of May, the three Combat Bombardment Wings had been expanded to a total of 11 groups, of which eight flew B-26s. As an indication of the intensity of operations, in the month of June 1944, the Ninth Air Force despatched 8,434 medium bomber sorties to occupied Europe, of which 6,405 attacked, dropping 12,030 tons of bombs and suffering the loss of 25 aircraft.

On June 6, 1944, as Allied armies poured ashore on the beaches of Normandy, the B-26s of the 323rd BG flew four missions within those 24 hours. Three were intended to pound the beach defenses and the last was to bomb a rail junction at Caen. On August 26, as the Allies pressed on across France, the 323rd moved from England to Lessay, in Normandy.

The D-Day targets for the 344th BG based at Stansted, in Essex, were coastal batteries at Cherbourg. These proved tough nuts to crack, and under an overcast the Marauders were forced to fly below 5,000ft to make their runs along the beaches. One B-26 exploded in mid-air following an attack by an Fw 190. Throughout the rest of

June, the group's bombers supported the taking of the Cotentin Peninsula and the British thrust against Caen. The 344th BG moved to Cormeilles-en-Vexin on September 30, joining the six other B-26 groups already in northern France.

Confronting this land and air onslaught were just under 1,000 Luftwaffe single-engined fighters rushed in from the Reich. Operating from barely prepared emergency strips, they struggled throughout June and July to make even a dent in the overwhelming Allied strength. Generalmajor Adolf Galland toured his units in the West at this time:

> My impressions were shattering. In addition to the appalling conditions, there was a far-reaching decline in morale. This feeling of irrevocable inferiority, the heavy losses, the hopelessness of the fighting, which had never before been so clearly demonstrated to us, the reproaches from above, the disrepute into which the Luftwaffe had fallen among the other arms of the forces from no fault of the individual, together with all the other burdens that the war at this stage had brought to every German, were the most severe test ever experienced by the Luftwaffe.

The *Staffelführer* of 9./JG 3, Leutnant Dieter Zink, told a fellow prisoner after he was shot down in his Bf 109 on July 11:

> Allied numerical superiority is quite colossal. You could say that their superiority in numbers is in the ratio of twenty-to-one, and then their materiel is better, and also their personnel. All our pilots are inexperienced, while theirs are all fairly experienced. Better aircraft too – but there's nothing we can do about that. We had to stand on our airfield

Marauders of the 17th BG pull away from a target, possibly a fuel or ammunition dump they have left ablaze, somewhere in southern Germany in April 1945. Photo via Ronnie Macklin. (Robert Forsyth Collection)

Positioned to defend the skies over northern Germany and the approach to Berlin from early 1945 were the Me 262s of the Luftwaffe's main interceptor unit, JG 7. Here, a pair of jets have been fitted with WGr. 21 rifled air-to-air mortar launching tubes – an installation that was neither common nor effective when fitted to the Me 262. (EN Archive)

looking up at the sky, watching them fly over. We had six aircraft on the ground ready for operations and they used to circle about up there with between 80 and 100 aircraft. To take off was suicidal.

As the Luftwaffe's situation deteriorated, so the Allied air forces grew stronger still. In November more USAAF and French B-26 Marauder units arrived in Europe as part of the First Tactical Air Force. These included the 17th BG, which came in from Corsica to Rouvres-en-Plaine, near Dijon. As the pincers closed on the Third Reich, Marauders of the First Tactical Air Force shared missions with their Ninth Air Force colleagues and those of the Twelfth Air Force.

From the fall of 1944, the Luftwaffe's prestige with Hitler sank to an all-time low – it seemed the *Jagdwaffe* was incapable of defending its home airspace or protecting Germany's factories and cities. Fighter losses were rising to nearly 30 percent of sorties flown, while victories gained amounted to less than 0.2 percent of Allied strength. Allied fighters virtually ruled the skies over Germany. Reichsmarschall Hermann Göring, the blusterous commander-in-chief of the Luftwaffe, had to act – and act he did.

For a long time Göring had been dissatisfied with Galland, and he saw him as the reason for the ailing performance of the fighter arm. The fact that since the summer Galland had been endeavoring to preserve and restrengthen the Reich-based *Jagdgeschwader* in order to deploy some 2,000 aircraft en masse in a knock-out blow against a major USAAF daylight raid was ignored. Training programs were established so that the home defense units would be able to respond quickly to any enemy air incursion. A network of emergency airfields was set up and communications between command centers and units was improved. Galland was prepared to sacrifice 400 aircraft and the lives of up to 150 precious pilots in order to bring down 400–500 heavy bombers in one so-called "*Grosse Schlag*" ("Great Blow"). Such aircraft attrition would mean the loss of 4,000–5,000 American aircrew, a blow from which even the USAAF would struggle to recover.

By November 1944 the largest number of fighters fielded by the Luftwaffe in the West since 1940, drawn from 11 *Geschwader* and supplemented by day fighters on the Western Front as well as some 100 night fighters in Denmark and southern Germany, was ready to take on the bombers.

In many respects, however, Galland's plans can be viewed as being unrealistic. His operation would have demanded high levels of coordination from large numbers of pilots whose abilities, in terms of training and experience, fell way short of the mark – such was the state of the fighter arm by this stage of the war. Furthermore, Galland did not bargain for Hitler's plans when, unexpectedly in December, he received news of the forthcoming offensive in the Ardennes. His fighters would thus be needed on the Western Front to support the impending campaign that was deceptively codenamed Operation *Watch on the Rhine*.

Over Christmas week of 1944, Galland embarked on a tour of western-based *Gruppen*. What he found shocked him:

> Units in the 3. *Jagddivision* area under [Generalmajor Walter] Grabmann were embittered about the leadership. The overall impression was shocking. I prepared a comprehensive report about my impressions, the mistakes made, and submitted my proposals. Everywhere I went I found shortcomings basically due to insufficient training and lack of experience on the part of the unit commanders. Added to this was the considerable indignation about the leadership's desultory manner of allocating responsibilities and expecting unit commanders to lead from their desks. My report explained the reasons, and why the *Jagdwaffe* received a deadly blow during the Ardennes offensive ending in Operation *Bodenplatte*.

Operation *Bodenplatte* was the surprise low-level attack against 21 enemy airfields in northwest Europe at dawn on January 1, 1945. A total of 271 Bf 109s and Fw 190s were lost in the raid, with a further 65 damaged. Some 143 pilots were killed or posted as missing, with a further 21 wounded and 70 captured. These figures included no fewer than 22 experienced unit leaders. Galland wrote in his diary, "An offensive in the West was senseless. I knew that the insufficient training and lack of experience of our unit commanders meant the *Jagdwaffe* was doomed to failure."

It was probably his Christmas report that sealed Galland's fate. On his own initiative, before the end of the month, he had requested the Luftwaffe Chief-of-Staff, General der Flieger Karl Koller, "to support my request for my return to operational service at the front." Shortly after, however, during the course of a "one-sided" two-and-a-half-hour telephone call from Göring, Galland was given the reasons why the Reichsmarschall had decided to sack him. Galland recorded in his diary:

> Göring tried to blame me without really having a clear opinion himself. Amongst other things, he reproached me for a negative influence on fighter tactics, a lack of support and failure to enforce orders, for having created my own empire in the fighter arm, wrong staff policy, the removal of people I did not like and my responsibility for the bad state of the *Jagdwaffe*.
>
> I was not permitted to say a word in my defense. At the end, Göring expressed his gratitude, saying that after my leave, he would appoint me to an important position within the leadership. I said that this was not acceptable since under no circumstances would I want to be in a leading position now that the *Jagdwaffe*'s collapse was imminent. I again requested to be employed operationally on the Me 262, not as a unit leader, but simply as a pilot. A decision was to be made during my leave.

Galland subsequently left for his enforced period of leave "embittered, depressed and without any definite plan for the future."

THE COMBATANTS

— B-26 MARAUDER CREW TRAINING

"The B-26 is a teamwork airplane." So proclaims the B-26 Pilot Training Manual of December 1944. The USAAF placed absolute priority on efficient and sufficient training for its aircrews fighting in overseas theaters of war. When it came to the B-26 Marauder, it was no different, but the 1944 manual made it clear that it was the responsibility of the "airplane commander" – the pilot – to ensure that his assigned crew functioned at maximum efficiency:

> Your success in combat and the safety of your crew and airplane depend on how well you organize and lead your crew during training. Your primary responsibility toward your crew is to see that every man is completely trained to take his place on the team. You are responsible for seeing that your team is capable of safe, efficient and successful conduct on all missions during training and combat operation. Supervise the training of the team both on the ground and in the air. Check their progress constantly. Consult with the supervisory personnel in charge of their training. Organize your own supplementary training program for yourself and your crew. You have only a short time to perfect the training of your crew, and to learn how to coordinate their jobs in the most efficient manner. The job must be done thoroughly. Use every available minute.

From 1942, standard USAAF policy was to bring a bomber crew together and "mold" it through a training process in the US before shipping it to the European Theater of Operations (ETO), MTO, or another theater.

Once a pilot had qualified to transition onto the Marauder, he was sent to a specialist B-26 Transitional Training Field at either MacDill Field in Tampa, Florida, or Barksdale Field in Shreveport, Louisiana. Here, trainees would endeavor to familiarize themselves with, and to eventually master, the Marauder,

A young 2Lt James L. Vining from Louisiana photographed during his preliminary pilot training in a PT-19A Cornell primary trainer in 1942–43. The low-wing, two-seat PT-19A was powered by a Fairchild Ranger 200hp L-440-3 engine. Vining would go on to fly B-26 Marauders with the 323rd BG, and on April 20, 1945 he would survive a devastating attack by Me 262s of JV 44. Photo via James Vining. (Robert Forsyth Collection)

despite many pilots – both instructors and pupils – having no previous twin-engined experience. Barksdale became known fondly as "The Country Club of the Air Corps" on account of its high standard of accommodation, a Postal Exchange, the amenities of a city nearby and, most importantly, decent food.

Later, two more transitional fields were set up at Laughlin Army Airfield at Del Rio in Texas and at Dodge City Army Airfield in Kansas, while MacDill and Barksdale became Operational Training Bases where entire bomb groups would train for operations in combat-ready B-26s. As the war progressed and more groups were formed, so Barksdale became a Replacement Training Base where new crews were trained to replace losses suffered in-theater. To Barksdale was added Lake Charles, Louisiana, Baer Field at Fort Wayne, Indiana, and Craig Field at Selma, Alabama. These bases also had satellite fields.

Despite the USAAF insisting on a high degree of organization and professionalism when it came to training crews destined to fly the Marauder at MacDill, the bomber suffered from an increasingly maligned reputation that saw it dubbed a "widow-maker" during the course of 1942 because of a high number of training crashes – the expression "one a day in Tampa Bay" haunted instructors and trainee crews alike. While Barksdale experienced crashes as well, in both cases the reality was more like "one a week."

One man who worked hard to overcome the negative aura surrounding the B-26 accident rate was Brig Gen James Doolittle, newly assigned to the embryonic Eighth Air Force, who applied pressure on the Army Air Safety Board and the Martin Company to sort the problem out once and for all. As a result of this, Martin sent teams of its own mechanics to the training fields to assist and provide instruction to USAAF personnel, and wherever possible at least one Martin mechanic was assigned to each squadron of 13 aircraft. Martin also set up a Service Training School at its Middle River plant to train USAAF mechanics specifically on the B-26, and by early 1944 7,000 men had been trained accordingly.

In a further initiative, Doolittle sent his technical adviser and pilot Capt Vincent W. Burnett to tour the Operational Training Bases and the Martin plants at Baltimore and Omaha. Whilst there, he performed reassuring demonstration flights in a B-26, including single-engined flight, slow flying, and recoveries from unusual and

1. Pilot deviation indicator gauge
2. Bomb release signal light
3. Compass
4. Turn-and-bank indicator
5. Rate of climb gauge
6. Gyro horizon
7. Torpedo director light rheostat
8. Manifold pressure gauge
9. Oil pressure gauge
10. RPM gauge (tachometer)
11. Oil temperature gauge
12. Fuel pressure gauge
13. Propeller check switches
14. Compass correction card holder
15. Altimeter
16. Suction gauge
17. Airspeed gauge
18. Landing gear and wing flap indicator

19. Marker beacon
20. Windshield wiper switch
21. Propeller anti-icer rheostat
22. Carburetor air temperature gauge
23. Cylinder head temperature gauge
24. Oil cooler and cowl flap gauge
25. Torpedo plug-in
26. Radio compass
27. Free air temperature gauge
28. De-icer gauge
29. Fuel gauge
30. Compass repeater
31. Pilot's control yoke
32. Co-pilot's control yoke
33. Rudder pedals
34. Rudder trim wheel
35. Propeller anti-icer rheostat
36. Elevator trim wheel

37. Ignition master switch
38. Flap control levers
39. Oil cooler control levers
40. Carburetor air control lever
41. Fluorescent light
42. Landing gear controls
43. Throttle controls
44. Propeller controls
45. Mixture controls
46. Cowl flaps controls
47. Blowers and guard
48. Intercom microphones
49. Interphone jack box
50. Radio compass control box
51. Command receiver control box
52. Pilot's seat
53. Co-pilot's seat

emergency flight situations. On two occasions, in front of groups of senior USAAF officers, Burnett flew a B-26 around the towers at both Martin factories, and then, having dived from altitude, flew at low-level with one engine cut and a propeller feathered.

Lt Paul M. Brady wanted to be a pilot. He had entered the Army Air Force Aviation Cadet Program in December 1942 in Boston, Massachusetts, which included basic training at the Atlantic City Training Center in New Jersey. Following completion of his basic training, he spent a six-month spell "marking time" with a College Training Detachment before being sent to the Air Force Classification Center in Nashville, Tennessee, where cadets underwent two weeks of intensive psychological and physical evaluation before being assigned to a specific flying crew role. As Brady described:

> Many a heart was broken there when the lists were finally posted as to which cadets were going on to Pilot Training and those who would be going on to Bombardier or Navigator Training.

Brady was fortunate enough to make the list for pilot training, and he was sent to Pre-Flight School at Maxwell Field in Montgomery, Alabama, followed by Primary Flight Training at Fletcher Field in Clarksdale, Mississippi. He then undertook Basic Flight Training at Greenville, Mississippi, and Multi-Engine Advanced Flight Training at George Field in Lawrenceville, Illinois:

> The later days of my advanced flight training conjured up a multitude of expectations as to where, after graduation, my multi-engine assignment would take me. Would it be to B-17s or B-24s and a European assignment? Or would it be in B-29s with an assignment in the Pacific? In my wildest imagination, I never expected that my after-graduation assignment would be to B-26s, with orders to report to Del Rio for further training.
>
> We had all heard about the bad reputation of the B-26 Martin Marauder, nicknamed the "Bee Dee Crash," "The Widow-Maker," and "The Baltimore Whore." I knew that this assignment would surely test my skills as a pilot, and I would be joining a rather elite group of airmen who were fast developing a reputation as being on the cutting edge of aviation.

The Marauder *was* a hot airplane and accidents were almost an everyday occurrence. For new graduates just out of flying school, the transition from an all-wood Beech AT-10 to a B-26 was a quantum leap in required flying skill levels that demanded extremely close attention to the aircraft's many aerodynamic idiosyncrasies.

After his transitional training at Laughlin Army Airfield, Brady was sent on to the Replacement Training Unit at Lake Charles, and from there he was eventually shipped to England, where he joined the 387th BG's 557th BS at Chipping Ongar, in Essex. In April 1945, he would experience at first-hand what it was like to come up against the Luftwaffe's Me 262 in combat.

The newly assigned crew of 2Lt Tom Lotina, photographed at the Replacement Training Unit at Lake Charles, Louisiana, on October 5, 1944, shortly before being shipped to Europe. Lotina is at far left, and next to him is his co-pilot, 2Lt Paul M. Brady. At far right is tail gunner SSgt Robert "Bob" M. Ferrara. The crew would be assigned to the 557th BS/ 387th BG, and on April 9, 1945 they would encounter Me 262s during a mission to bomb an ordnance depot at Amberg-Kummersbruck. Photo via Tom Lotina. (Robert Forsyth Collection)

Tail gunner SSgt Bob Ferrara, who would also encounter the Me 262 in the ETO, recalled his time at the Miami Beach Training Center in Florida in 1944:

Most of my fellow recruits wanted to be pilots, but I was the only one who really wanted to be a tail gunner. I chose Armament School and learned everything I could about the 0.50-cal. machine gun. The school [run by the Air Corps Technical School] was at Lowry Field in Denver, Colorado.

Never having seen a real gun in my life, I was quite amazed when I got my first machine gun in order to study its parts, functions and malfunctions. One day during a break, I said to a buddy that I wanted to be the best gunner in the air force. After three months of armament school they shipped me to three months of gunnery school at Fort Myers, Florida.

Accommodation was basic, and Ferrara remembers how trainees complained that the coops provided for the chickens were better than the housing provided for the men.

Trainees qualified for marksmanship using 0.45-cal. pistols, and they would spend days stripping down and rebuilding the 0.50-cal. Browning AN/M2 machine gun until, quite literally, they could do it blindfolded. Ferrara initially failed his end of course first test and his dreams of being a tail gunner began to fade. "I cried like a baby

The men of the new 34th BS/ 17th BG line up in front of one the Marauders at the B-26 Transitional Training Field at Barksdale Field in Shreveport, Louisiana, on August 8, 1942. At this time the unit was being strengthened almost daily with the arrival of newly qualified personnel. The lessons they had learned during their training would be of vital importance in the skies over Europe in the years ahead. Photo via Ronnie Macklin. (Robert Forsyth Collection)

at night and my buddies thought I was cuckoo for wanting to be a tail gunner." But he was given a second chance and passed:

> I was the happiest guy in camp. Now we were ready to use all the things we had learned at armament and gunnery schools. The trainees went for their first flight in a B-17 bomber at 20,000ft and fired live ammo at a drone towed by a small plane. Five gunners would make a flight together, and we were crammed in the nose section.

An hour later, Ferrara was informed that his fire had shattered the target in a way not seen before. By using ammunition painted in different colors, instructors could tell how each gunner had scored. Aside from practical instruction, there was also a classroom element, as Ferrara described:

> We spent five straight days viewing slides of German, English and American aircraft. They were shown on the screen for just a fraction of a second. Believe it or not, it became easy to identify the planes instantly.

In the December 1944 B-26 training manual, pilots were informed that:

> Your armorer-gunner is the hardest man in your crew to keep busy in flight. Your training curriculum calls for only a limited number of practice gunnery missions, but nothing prevents you from having your gunner practice turret operation and sighting and aiming at every opportunity. Because of his lack of other duties, he has more time for this sort of practice than any other member of the crew.
>
> See that he spends plenty of time in the squadron armament section. He can learn much through helping the regular armament personnel install and load guns, repair and service turrets, and doing general shop work.

With the arrival of B-26s in England in March 1943, VIII Bomber Command decreed that new crews for the "mediums" should be sent to the Combat Crew Replacement Center (CCRC) at Bovingdon, in Hertfordshire, where they would mix with crews allocated for B-17s and B-24s. But as the Marauder force expanded, additional groups arrived and combat operations commenced, so a new, dedicated center in the form of the 2902nd CCRC Group (Bombardment) (Provisional) was established in August 1943 at Toome in Northern Ireland, although it did not open until September 20, functioning alongside the 2905th Replacement and Training Squadron.

For practice flying, Toome received the initial "short-wing" B-26Bs used by

The crew of 2Lt James L. Stalter (far left) photographed at the completion of their training at Lake Charles. On April 24, 1945, while piloting B-26G-1 43-34181 *Lak-a-Nookie* of the 495th BS/344th BG, Stalter witnessed the Me 262A-1a of Oberst Günther Lützow of JV 44 being pursued by a P-47 of the 365th FG during a mission to Schrobenhausen. Photo via James Stalter. (Robert Forsyth Collection)

1Lt John W. Sorrelle (far left) flew the April 26, 1945 mission to Schrobenhausen as the pilot of a B-26 of the 432nd BS/17th BG. During the course of this sortie his engineer-gunner, TSgt Cleo Wills (fourth from left), opened fire on an Me 262, and in doing so could well have damaged Generalleutnant Adolf Galland's aircraft. The crew are seen here upon the completion of combat crew training at Barksdale Field in August 1944. Photo via John Sorrelle. (Robert Forsyth Collection)

the 322nd BG, and by November there were 32 B-26s and four A-20 Havocs on strength and more than 50 crews training. This process was handled by the Eighth Air Force, despite the fact that B-26s were being transferred to the Ninth Air Force from October. This process continued until the disbandment of the CCRCs in September 1944.

In 1944, the USAAF's First Motion Picture Unit made "*How to Fly the B-26 Airplane*", a well-produced 47-minute instructional film on the Marauder which was "dedicated to helping [the pilot] use it surpassingly well." Actor Don Porter, who plays the part of the pilot, experiences a mock engine failure while airborne. His handling of this provides would-be Marauder crews with further instruction on the aircraft's emergency landing procedure.

Me 262A-1a

It was an irony of war that just as Germany had developed, manufactured, and sent into action the world's first operational jet interceptor in the fall of 1944, the Third Reich's ability to sustain its deployment was already eroding. By the end of that year, with Me 262s now being delivered in significant numbers, as a result of growing shortages in fuel, aircraft, and instructors, as well as increasingly adverse operating conditions, the Luftwaffe became almost incapable of sustaining an organized and structured training program for the jet fighter with which it hoped to win back some degree of air superiority.

In the fall of 1944, 10.*Staffel* of III./EJG 2 was formed at Lechfeld. The intention was to establish a dedicated Me 262 operational training unit which would offer pilots converting to the jet comprehensive and thorough tuition. The unit was helped by the appointment of Oberstleutnant Heinz Bär, one of the Luftwaffe's most renowned fighter aces and leaders, as its commander. His operational career stretched back to 1939, and subsequently after service on all major fronts, he was credited with more than 190 victories and awarded the Swords and Oak Leaves to the Knight's Cross. However, earlier in 1944, he had clashed with Göring, and his appointment to III./EJG 2 was seen as being sidelined to some extent.

Initially, about 50 pilots were assembled from fighter and bomber units and fighter school staffs, and a selection was made of promising new pilots who were about halfway through their operational fighter training. The new pilots were given a pre-jet flying course which consisted of finishing their regular 20 hours flying time in conventional fighter aircraft with the throttles fixed in one position to reproduce a technical problem found in flying in the Me 262, the throttles of which were not to be adjusted in flight at high altitudes.

ROBERT M. FERRARA

Robert "Bob" M. Ferrara was born to Italian parents in Needham, Massachusetts, on August 25, 1925, his father a shoemaker. He was the last of the children to be born into the family and, tragically, his mother died giving birth to him. During the years of the Great Depression, the family moved to Portland, Maine, so that his father could maintain a living, and Robert was brought up mainly by his sisters.

Ferrara was 16 years old when the Japanese bombed Pearl Harbor. His older brother subsequently joined the USAAF and served as a tail gunner in a B-26 in North Africa. The story was that his crew "had to steal gas to fly missions." Ferrara always believed that he would be a tail gunner and, as a "proud, patriotic American teenager," , prioritized enlistment above his school work. His father told him that if he was not going to study properly he should join the army. He hitchhiked from Portland to Boston in order to enlist in the US Marine Corps, but was turned down because of a minor birth deformity. Subsequently, Ferrara enlisted in the USAAF at Fort Devens, Massachusetts, shortly after his 18th birthday in 1943. He was then sent to the Miami Beach Training Center for basic training:

It was 94 degrees, and I had never been so hot in my life. We were put in a beautiful hotel with three men to a room. Most of my fellow recruits wanted to be pilots, but I was the only one who really wanted to be a tail gunner. I chose Armament School and learned everything I could about the 0.50-cal. machine gun.

Ferrara attended the Armament School at Lowry Field, which was run by the Air Corps Technical School. Three months later he was posted to the school for flexible gunnery at Fort Myers. After another three months, and with

Cpl Robert "Bob" M. Ferrara, newly qualified as an air gunner. Photo via Otto Kammerdiener. (Robert Forsyth Collection)

the rank of corporal, he was moved for Transitional Training at Barksdale Field, where he spent several weeks training on the B-26 and was assigned to the crew of Lt Tom Lotina. After training was completed, he and his crew were sent to New York, from where they would leave for England by ship in an escorted convoy in late October 1944. "We made the Atlantic crossing in an English transport. The food was awful and the ship was filthy. We spent half our time on deck because most of the men were seasick."

Once in England, Bob and his crew were assigned to the 557th BS of the 387th BG, based at Chipping Ongar.

One of the Luftwaffe's most accomplished fighter aces and unit commanders, Oberstleutnant Heinz Bär was appointed to lead the Me 262 training and conversion *Gruppe* III./EJG 2 based at Lechfeld. This assignment was seen as something of a demotion, as Bär had fallen foul of Göring who transferred him away from frontline command. He is seen here at Lechfeld on the wing of his Me 262 "Red 13". Bär's final posting would be as operational commander of JV 44, replacing the wounded Galland. (EN Archive)

Upon arrival at Lechfeld, all pilots were given three days theoretical instruction in the operation and functioning of jet engines, the features and flying qualities of the Me 262, as well as some practice in operating the controls in a wingless training model. The RLM also commissioned a 40-minute instructional film on how to fly the Me 262, featuring a pair of actors who, respectively, played an officer instructor and an NCO pupil who had previously served together in Africa. The actors work through pre-flight check sequences, after which Me 262 "White 10" takes off and is seen in flight with the pupil at the controls. Then, from the ground, the pupil is instructed to shut down one turbine so as to experience flight on one engine. Things go successfully, and as with the aforementioned B-26 instructional "movie," the film draws to a close with a friendly cigarette and a chat between instructor and pupil.

The "classroom" introduction was followed by a course at Landsberg in the operation of conventional twin-engined aircraft. Pupils were given five hours flying time in a Bf 110 and an Si 204, practicing take-offs, landings, flight with the radio course indicator, instrument flying, and flying on one engine. Upon completion of the course, the pilots returned to III./EJG 2 at Lechfeld, where they were given one more day of theoretical instruction and then began conversion to the Me 262.

Practical instruction on the Me 262 began with a half-day's exercise in starting and stopping the jet motors and taxiing. Flying instruction consisted of a total of nine take-offs to familiarize the pilot with fuel flow, aerobatics, high altitude operations, aerial maneuvers, formation flying, and gunnery practice. This was considered to be the minimum with which to qualify a pilot for operational readiness on the Me 262.

By late November 1944, a number of pilots considered to have sufficient aptitude for flying the jet interceptor were sent initially to 9./EJG 2 at Landsberg, where they undertook preparatory training. This involved four-and-a-half hours spent practicing on twin-engined Si 204s and Bf 110s with a further six hours on a Bü 181 for gunnery and target skills. Successful candidates were then transferred to Unterschlauersbach for final conversion, with the training at this time consisting of:

- Circuits – three starts/1.5 hours
- Altitude flights (39,370 ft) – two starts/two hours
- Navigation training – one start/45 minutes
- Formation flying – one start/30 minutes

Me 262A-1a "Red S," possibly of JV 44, is readied for flight at Brandenburg-Briest in March 1945. This aircraft is also believed to have been used for hurried training of more experienced pilots making the transition from single-engined piston fighters to the twin-engined jet interceptor. Note the generator cart and fire extinguisher to the left of the Me 262 and the parachute lying on its port wing. (EN Archive)

Throughout December, the number of pilots undergoing training at Lechfeld increased dramatically in proportion to the instructors – a total of 135 trainee pilots for only 28 instructors, and the ratio of aircraft to pilots was even lower. Training was severely restricted due to a shortage of two-seat Me 262B-1 trainers, and even by the end of January 1945, III./EJG 2 recorded only three such machines on strength.

Major Erich Hohagen was a 55-victory ace who had seen combat over the Channel Front and in the Soviet Union with JG 2 and JG 27. He was posted to III./EJG 2 in late 1944, prior to taking command of the embryonic Me 262 *Gruppe*, III./JG 7. He recalled:

Major Erich Hohagen sits in the cockpit of an Me 262 of III./EJG 2 whilst undergoing conversion onto the fighter at Lechfeld in late 1944. Awarded the Knight's Cross in October 1941, Hohagen was one of the *Jagdwaffe*'s most experienced unit commanders by the time he joined JV 44. He is strapped into the self-contained "*Wanne*" ("tub") sub-assembly, which held the instrument panel and electrical controls, stick and rudder, throttles, seat, and battery. (EN Archive)

I had only received one week's training on the Me 262 at Lechfeld, as far as I remember, but I was very proud and honored to fly it since I was still suffering from a head fracture that had occurred one month before. It was the absolute fulfilment of my flying career, and I knew for sure that, at that time, no further enhancements could be made. It was the biggest step since the Wright brothers flew an aircraft heavier than air. Basically, there was no similarity in flight characteristics compared to other aircraft I had flown, and though it was easier to handle on the piloting part, things were much more critical on the flight safety side of things. For example, the engines could have been improved and better fatigue resistance built in. I also felt that the hydraulic system was insufficient and that there would have been benefit from the installation of dive brakes.

It was a similar experience for Leutnant Walter Hagenah, who had shot down nine enemy bombers while flying the Fw 190. He recounted:

We were not even allowed to look inside the cowling of the jet engines because we were told that they were secret and we did not "need to know" what was there! Our "ground school" lasted for about one

1. Airspeed indicator
2. Artificial horizon
3. Variometer
4. Altimeter
5. Radio Compass
6. SZKK-2 ammunition counter
7. Tachometers
8. Exhaust gas temperature gauges
9. Fuel injection pressure gauges
10. Fuel gauges
11. Cockpit heat control
12. Fuel counters
13. Engine starter switches
14. Gun camera switch
15. Free air temperature gauge
16. Hydraulic pressure gauge

17. Nose wheel brake
18. Ventilator control
19. Vertical speed indicator
20. Turn-and-bank indicator
21. Oil pressure gauge
22. AFN-2 radio navigation/homing indicator
23. Clock
24. Revi 16b gunsight
25. Oxygen flow meter
26. Oxygen contents gauge
27. Emergency landing gear handle
28. Emergency flaps handle
29. Horizontal stabilizer trim control
30. Horizontal stabilizer trim indicator
31. Landing gear indicator lights
32. Fuel shut-off selector lever

33. Throttle controls
34. Oxygen control valve
35. Main light switch
36. Rudder pedals
37. Control column
38. Pilot's seat
39. Canopy release lever
40. Switches panel
41. Windshield heater switch
42. Flare release switch
43. Bomb release handle
44. Bomb control panel
45. Circuit breaker test panel
46. FuG 25 IFF panel

afternoon. We were told about the peculiarities of the jet engine, the danger of a flame-out at high altitude and the poor acceleration at low altitude. Then we were told of the vital importance of handling the throttles carefully or else the engine might catch fire.

On the day before my first flight in the Me 262, I had a brief flight in a Si 204 to practice twin-engine handling and asymmetric flying. Next morning, March 25, 1945, I made my first familiarization flight in the rear seat of a two-seat Me 262B – precisely 17 minutes – accompanied by a weapons technician/instructor from Brandenburg-Briest. I was greatly impressed by the Me 262.

The take-off was easy, the visibility from the cockpit was marvelous after the tail-down Bf 109 and Fw 190, and there was no torque during take-off. The only real problem I found was that when I came into land, I came in at normal speed, expecting the speed to fall away rapidly when the throttle was closed. But the Me 262 was such a clean machine. We had been warned before take-off not to throttle back to less than 6,000rpm – we were also told, when turning on the base leg for landing, not to do so at less than 300km/h. The important thing was to make up your mind in good time whether you were going to land or throw away that approach and try another. If you throttled back and the engine revolutions fell too low, they would not accelerate quickly enough if you tried to open up and go round again.

Brandenburg-Briest had a concrete runway and jets could set fire to tarmac! Once you began to exceed 900 km/h, the Me 262 did not "feel right." You did not have complete control of it as it drifted from side to side, and there was the feeling you would lose control if you took it much faster.

Generally, training was unbelievably short – just an afternoon's chat and a short morning's accompanied flight, then, in the afternoon, one went solo. We had some pilots with only about 100 hours total flying time on our unit flying the Me 262. Whilst they might have been able to take-off and land the aircraft, I had the definite impression that they would have been little use in combat.

But if things were rudimentary at Lechfeld, by early April 1945, in general, Me 262 training had become at best "hurried" and at worst almost non-existent. One example of this was the experience of Hauptmann Walter Krupinski. Far from being a novice, Krupinski had flown more than 1,100 operational missions, during which he had been credited with 197 confirmed victories. He had also been wounded five times, bailed out on four occasions, and undergone numerous crash-landings. By March 1945, Krupinski, a recipient of the Knight's Cross with Oak Leaves, had effectively been made redundant by the continual regroupings and redesignations of the various Luftwaffe fighter *Geschwader*. He duly joined JV 44, where his "training" on the Me 262 began in earnest on April 2, 1945 at Riem. A lone Me 262 was hauled out onto the concrete start platform on the western edge of the airfield. Oberst Johannes Steinhoff, Operations Officer of JV 44, was his "instructor." Krupinski remembers:

That morning I sat in the cockpit of an Me 262 at Riem. I had a hell of a bad head, the result of too many drinks the night before! Steinhoff was standing on the port wing. He said, "The most difficult thing with this type of aircraft is to start the engines. I'll do that for you."

High-scoring ace Hauptmann Walter Krupinski had flown more than 1,100 operational missions by the time he converted onto the Me 262 under the guidance of Oberst Johannes Steinhoff, Operations Officer of JV 44, at Riem on April 2, 1945. Credited with 197 aerial victories, Krupinski claimed two B-26s destroyed as his final successes. (EN Archive)

There was no reading any books or anything like that. There was no "training program." He just gave me some basic information, enough to get started. "It's very tricky," he said. "On take-off, you need a very long time until you get airborne. Don't do anything in a hurry. On landing, it's the other way around – you can't get the speed back down to a normal landing speed. She's fast, very fast!" Actually, I found that taking off in the Me 262 was fairly easy because the nose wheel rolled nice and smoothly, but the problem, as Steinhoff had said, was that the engines didn't accelerate and bring up speed fast enough. You needed the whole length of the airfield before you reached an adequate take-off speed. At Riem, the strip we used was about 1,100m long, and only after about 1,000m did you have the lifting speed to come off the field.

Anyway, I prepared myself for take-off. I closed the canopy, threw a quick glance over the instrument panel. Brakes off. Slowly, like a lame duck, the bird began to roll. But then the end of the runway, as I predicted, came towards me very quickly. A glance at the speed indicator told me I was moving at 200km/h. Pulling gently at the stick, I got into the air. No drag, and she climbed swiftly. Landing-gear up. Throttle lightly back to 8,000rpm. I climbed and the speed grew and grew – 350… 400… 500… 600 km/h – there seemed no end to its speed. Still I climbed. It was fantastic! Nothing like the Bf 109.

For my first roll in the climb I used only ailerons, moving with lightning speed – neither rudder nor thrust were needed, and at 6,000 or 7,000m I leveled out, the speed slowly approaching 900km/h. So there I was, flying on my first mission, though I suppose it was more of a solo transition flight really.

Another experienced fighter ace to fly the Me 262 from March 1945 who underwent similar "training" to Krupinski was Oberleutnant Walter Schuck, one of the most successful pilots with JG 5 in the Far North. He had been awarded the Knight's Cross on April 8, 1944 in recognition of his 84 victories, with the Oak Leaves following on September 30. He later joined JG 7. When Schuck asked Steinhoff how the Me 262 conversion program was organized, he was told to "Go and stand outside next to the runway and watch how the others do it!"

After several days of carefully watching and studying how the jets were handled, Schuck climbed into an Me 262 and received a brief run-through from one of his more-experienced comrades on the aircraft's instruments, operating procedures and idiosyncrasies. Schuck then took off on his first flight. He found the performance of the jet astonishing. Sometime later, safely back on the ground, he emerged from the cockpit with his knees shaking and his overalls soaked in sweat.

Just how effective or successful these hasty attempts at training the Luftwaffe's pilots on the jet interceptor were would be proved in the skies over Germany in the last three months of the war.

OTTO KAMMERDIENER

Otto Kammerdiener was typical of the small band of qualified NCO instructor pilots who flew the Me 262 operationally, albeit briefly, with JV 44 in 1945. He was born on July 23, 1921 in the Altona district of Hamburg and joined the Luftwaffe at the age of 18 in November 1939, two months after war was declared. Kammerdiener was assigned to 3./*Fliegerausbildungsregiment* (Flying Training Regiment) 13 in Neubiberg. After his initial period of basic fitness and infantry training, as well as team sports, he passed his medical examinations and spent a short time with 1.*Technisches Kompanie* (Technical Company) of the *Fliegerwaffentechnische Schule* (*See*) (Maritime Aerial Armament Technical School) under Oberstleutnant Heinz von Holleben at Büg on the island of Rügen off the Pomeranian coast.

Kammerdiener had been posted to Büg with the aim of a career in the Luftwaffe's maritime flying arm. Between April–August 1940 he was based at Heiligenhafen, on the Baltic coast, serving with 6.*Fliegerausbildungsbataillon* (Aviation Training Battalion) 26 under Oberst Erich Boenisch, before heading to Pütnitz to join the *Flugzeugführerschule* (FFS) (*See*) (Marine Pilot Training School). Then, in December 1940, with the rank of gefreiter, Kammerdiener progressed to FFS A/B 119 at Jüterbog-Damm under Oberstleutnant Rudolf Behm, where he undertook more advanced pilot training, including aerobatics, instrument instruction, formation, and cross-country flying.

Promoted from unteroffizier to feldwebel on April 1, 1943, Kammerdiener was sent to Quedlinburg, a satellite base of the *Fluglehrerschule* (Flight Leader School) at Brandenburg-Briest, in July of that year. Here, he trained to be an

Gefreiter Otto Kammerdiener (right) during advanced pilot training. Photo via Otto Kammerdiener. (Robert Forsyth Collection)

instructor, and following qualification he was assigned to Brandenburg-Briest in August 1944. By this time the *Fluglehrerschule* was providing preliminary training to fighter pilots on Ar 96s and Si 204s. However, because of the war situation, his instructing days would be relatively brief, for within eight months, on March 11, 1945, he joined JV 44, which was forming up at Brandenburg-Briest and with whom he would fly the Me 262A-1a in combat.

COMBAT

By late March 1945, the Luftwaffe's newest Me 262 fighter unit was in the final stages of forming up at Brandenburg-Briest, some 30 miles to the west of Berlin. Unlike the other principal Me 262 unit, JG 7, which was defending northern Germany and the airspace around the Berlin capital from attacks by the Eighth Air Force's "strategic" bombers, JV 44 was considerably smaller in size – not much larger than *Staffel*-strength. Indeed, by the end of the month, JV 44 had only some 20 pilots and around the same number of jet interceptors, as well as a pair of twin-engined Si 204s used for courier and liaison work.

On March 31, the OKL listed just nine Me 262s as having been delivered to the unit from the factories, and one of these jets was undergoing repair. Of the few aircraft that had been on strength already, six were unserviceable due to enemy air attacks on Briest. Just two more Me 262s were expected to be handed over by the training units at some point. By comparison, JG 7 reported 79 of its jets as serviceable on that date.

Irrespective of the small number of aircraft assigned to JV 44, it was remarkable in itself that the unit had progressed this far, for it had been created under an atmosphere of suspicion and exile. To a great extent the *Jagdverband* had been left to its own

Groundcrew attend to six of JV 44's Me 262A-1as lined up at their dispersal at Munich-Riem in April 1945. (Robert Forsyth Collection)

devices, and thus it hardly figured on many official reports, and many of its key personnel were considered as either no longer fit for combat or outcasts, and thus of no status in the eyes of the Luftwaffe leadership.

Yet what made JV 44 unusual in composition was its leadership. At the head of the *Jagdverband* was the recently sacked former commanding general of the *Jagdwaffe*, Generalleutnant Adolf Galland – a cigar-chomping, charismatic and accomplished fighter ace, once a darling of the German media, but now dismissed and, if Reichsmarschall Göring had his way, disgraced. But despite Göring's charges of mismanagement on the part of Galland, and some Machiavellian connivance on the part of a competing clique of officers, Galland still held influence over and had loyal friends amongst the Luftwaffe's senior fighter commanders.

The commander of JV 44, Generalleutnant Adolf Galland (right), together with Oberst Günther Lützow at Munich-Riem in April 1945. Between them, these two veteran fighter aces, whose operational flying careers stretched back to the Spanish Civil War, were credited with around 215 aerial victories. Both would end their Luftwaffe service flying the Me 262. Galland survived, Lützow did not. (Robert Forsyth Collection)

Throughout January 1945, by means of semi-covert meetings with a number of Luftwaffe generals and even senior SS officers, this small group of officers under Oberst Günther Lützow "mutinied" against Göring, attempting to force a meeting with him at which they intended to put forward their grievances about the unsatisfactory way the fighter arm was being run, and to demand Galland's reinstatement. This initiative proved unsuccessful.

Despite his fall from grace, Galland was given permission to set up his own semi-autonomous unit equipped with Me 262s and to take the "mutineers" with him. By March, JV 44 had been established at Brandenburg-Briest essentially to "prove" to the higher authorities that the Me 262 was an effective jet interceptor rather than a high-speed bomber, the latter role conforming to Hitler's vision of the aircraft, and to which, of course, Göring was compelled to subscribe.

In its formative phase, the unit numbered a handful of Luftwaffe fighter aces including the former *Kommodore* of JG 77 and JG 7, and holder of the Knight's Cross with Oak Leaves and Swords, Oberst Johannes Steinhoff. By February 1945, he is believed to have had 170 confirmed aerial victories. As a leading member of the "plot" against Göring, Steinhoff had been relieved of his command of JG 7. Galland also had Major Erich Hohagen, along with another Knight's Cross-holder, Major Karl-Heinz Schnell from JG 102, who was credited with more than 60 victories, Oberfeldwebel Klaus Neumann also from JG 7 with 19 four-engined bomber victories, and Oberfeldwebel Franz Steiner from 2./JG 11 with 12 victories, ten of which were four-engined bombers. The unit was further strengthened by a cadre of very experienced NCO flying instructors.

Most of March was taken up with preparing the unit, flying being confined to the Si 204s in order to instruct pilots in twin-engined take-offs and landings, instrument flying and radio familiarization. It would not be until March 14 that JV 44 took delivery of its first Me 262s, and the unit's first combat mission is believed to have

To date, Me 262A-1a Wk-Nr 111745 "White 5" is the most photographed of JV 44's jets. It took part in several operational sorties against USAAF medium bombers, and in terms of color scheme and finish the aircraft was very representative of the core force of Messerschmitts used by the unit. It is seen here at JV 44's dispersal area at the edge of Riem airport. At the time this shot was taken, the aircraft had not been fitted with racks for R4Ms. (EN Archive)

The transition from training to combat – the crew of 1Lt Tom Lotina (back row, right) of the 557th BS/387th BG photographed shortly after returning from a mission to bomb an ordnance depot at Amberg-Kummersbruck on April 9, 1945. Their appearance is very different from that of the fresh-faced crew photographed at Lake Charles seven months earlier (see the previous chapter). Tail gunner SSgt Bob Ferrara stands next to Lotina, while co-pilot 2Lt Paul Brady kneels in the front row, center. (Michael O'Leary)

been carried out towards the end of the month. Steinhoff learned two lessons from this mission. Firstly, that the Me 262 required a fine balance of speed and marksmanship, particularly in using its slow rate-of-fire nose-mounted 30mm MK 108 cannon, and secondly, that the aircraft consumed fuel quickly.

In the meantime, because the industries in Germany's southeastern cities such as Nuremburg, Munich, Augsburg, and Regensburg did not enjoy sufficient jet protection, Galland was ordered to relocate his unit south. He selected the modern civil airport of Riem, on the western edge of Munich, as his base, and on March 31 JV 44 flew south from Briest to its new zone of operations.

By this stage of the war, Riem had been transformed to operate Luftwaffe aircraft and personnel. It was a sprawling facility with an underground fuel store close to the largest of the two main hangars, the frontage of which spanned nearly 400m and the rear of which contained nine workshops. Aircraft could be sheltered in up to 35 large, purpose-built blast pens located off the north and south perimeter roads, and the airport was ringed with Flak emplacements. For the coming month, this would be the base from which JV 44 would engage the USAAF's B-26s.

By then, the Allied armies were advancing at up to 50 miles per day into Germany, and American forces had surrounded the Ruhr. British Prime Minister Winston Churchill felt that the war would be over within two months.

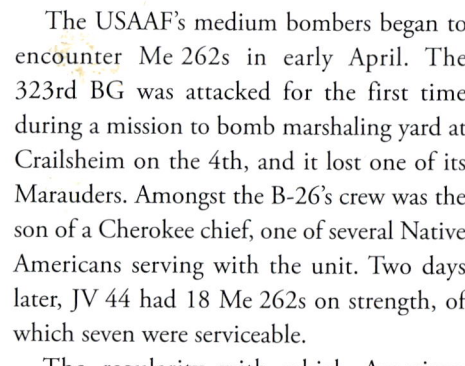

The USAAF's medium bombers began to encounter Me 262s in early April. The 323rd BG was attacked for the first time during a mission to bomb marshaling yard at Crailsheim on the 4th, and it lost one of its Marauders. Amongst the B-26's crew was the son of a Cherokee chief, one of several Native Americans serving with the unit. Two days later, JV 44 had 18 Me 262s on strength, of which seven were serviceable.

The regularity with which American "mediums" were striking targets was becoming relentless – on April 8 they dropped 843 tons of bombs on marshaling yards and oil storage facilities, although two bombers were lost and 44 damaged. At Nienhagen, B-26s from the 387th, 394th, and 397th BGs targeted the oil

Me 262A-1a R4M *ORKAN* ROCKET

In addition to its nose-mounted 30mm cannon, the Me 262A-1a could be fitted with a pair of wooden EG.-R4M racks with channels for loading 12 55mm R4M *Orkan* air-to-air rockets. The latter was a solid fuel-propelled, fin-stabilized missile that boasted a high charge weight to case weight ratio. The fuze was designed to discriminate between thin skin and more substantial main aircraft structure, and to penetrate 60–100cm into a target aircraft before detonation to give maximum blast effect. It was calculated that the loss of speed incurred by an Me 262 as a result of a launch rack being fitted was approximately 10mph. It had been expected to obtain an 80 percent kill score at 1,640–1,970ft.

refinery, causing smoke so dense that many Marauders had to make repeated bomb runs to ensure they had dropped their ordnance accurately. That afternoon a communications centre at Sonderhausen was attacked. The next day, B-26s from the 322nd, 323rd and 349th BGs bombed a munitions dump at Naumberg during the morning, leaving the target burning. In the afternoon, Marauders of the 323rd, and 344th BGs joined Invaders and Havocs to hit the marshaling yard at Saalfeld.

On April 11 the 9th Bombardment Division despatched 678 medium bombers to the marshaling yards at Aschersleben, Bernberg, Köthen, Rendorf, and Zwickau. Ammunition storage dumps at Naumberg and Bamberg were also targeted, and at the latter town bombing left 12 rail lines cut, rolling stock destroyed, buildings wrecked, and most of the marshaling yards unusable.

It is possible that JV 44 made its first significant attack against B-26s on the 16th when Galland led a formation of Me 262s equipped with new 55mm R4M air-to-air rockets against Marauders almost certainly from the 322nd BG, which lost two aircraft. British radio intercepts state that a formation of 14 jets of "an unidentified command (presumably south Germany) operated against B-26s." The 323rd BG sent

Marauders of the 34th BS/17th BG warm their engines prior to departing for a mission from Dijon during the winter of 1944–45. The nearest aircraft is B-26G-10 43-34461 *JOMAR*, assigned to pilot 1Lt Guy F. Nicklous. Parked next to it B-26B-40 42-43311 *SPOT CASH!*, which fell to the guns of an Me 262 from JV 44 on April 26, 1945 whilst being flown by 2Lt Earl E. Reeves – the Marauder was hit in both engines and its tail blown off. A gunner in an adjacent B-26 recalled, "I saw a big flash and I turned the turret to about 'three o'clock'. I realized the other B-26 at the right of us had gone. The Me 262 had blown it right out of the sky." (USAF)

its Marauders to bomb Kempten that day – a target that was well within range of the Me 262s at Riem – but none of the 323rd's distinctively marked "white-tailed" B-26s were claimed by JV 44 pilots as having been shot down.

On April 17 Me 262s of JV 44 were scrambled to engage incursions by medium bombers targeting yet more marshaling yards, oil storage facilities, and ordnance depots in southern Germany. At 1334 hrs, Galland led a formation of seven jets, including aircraft flown by Steinhoff and Krupinski, against B-26s most likely from the 17th and 320th BGs that had been tasked with bombing the ammunition dump at Altendettelsau, west of Nuremberg. The Me 262s were routed north via Ansbach, Rottenberg, and Nuremberg.

However, problems hampered the operation from the start. Oberfeldwebel Rudolf Nielinger, a former instructor from JG 103 and a veteran of II./JG 51 with 20 victories who had flown over the USSR and North Africa, was forced to turn back on account of defective landing gear. Unteroffizier Eduard Schallmoser, freshly trained by III./EJG 2, found that his EZ 42 gyroscopic gunsight was faulty. Nevertheless, he pressed on into the midst of the Marauders, only to discover that his MK 108 cannon had jammed. He banked around for a second pass, and was able to "unjam" his guns just in time to hit one of the P-47 escort fighters, although not without sustaining damage to his Messerschmitt. Although the Me 262 was left with a large hole in the canopy, somehow Schallmoser remained unharmed.

SSgt James A. Valimont, a tail gunner from the 34th BS/17th BG, was seriously wounded when the tail section of his B-26 was shot away during what was described as an "aggressive" attack by the Me 262s. His left leg was badly cut by flying fragments and only the framework of the Marauder's tail assembly remained intact. Nevertheless, according to the subsequent citation for his Distinguished Flying Cross, Valimont "resolutely manned his guns and on the next attack so badly damaged the fighter that the attack was diverted without further action."

The 17th BG had operated B-26s since mid-1942 when the group exchanged its B-25s for Marauders. From November 1942, the unit operated as part of the Twelfth Air Force in Algeria, flying "short-wing" B-26Bs in attacks on marshaling yards and airfields in Tunisia, and even conducting occasional anti-shipping missions. By early 1943 the 17th was the only B-26 group left in the MTO, and it carried out attacks both in North Africa and over Sardinia.

The unit remained in the Mediterranean, striking targets in Italy, carrying out low-level attacks on bridges and rail yards, and undertaking "Nickelling" – USAAF slang for leaflet drops. In August 1944 the group provided bombing support during the Allied landings in southern France. In September, the 17th operated from Poretta, on Corsica, striking targets in northern Italy, especially bridges in the Po Valley.

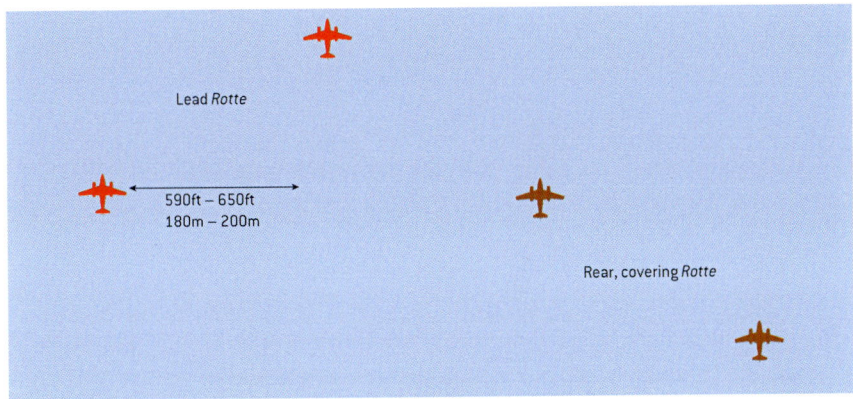

Lead *Rotte*

590ft – 650ft
180m – 200m

Rear, covering *Rotte*

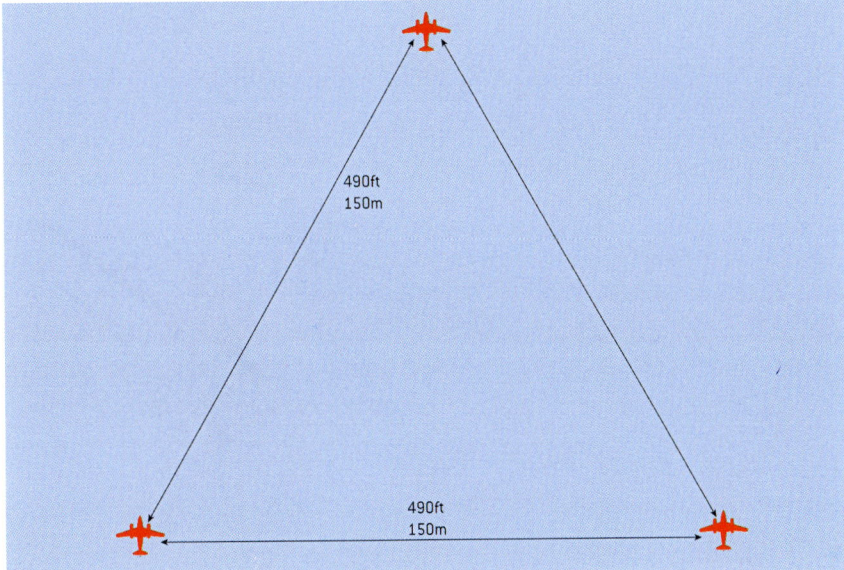

490ft
150m

490ft
150m

TOP

The standard four-aircraft *Schwarm* fighter formation evolved from the earlier three-aircraft *Kette*, as used by pilots of the *Legion Condor* during the Spanish Civil War and later favored by the Me 262 for tactical flexibility. The *Schwarm* comprised two *Rotten* in which one wingman, positioned behind, monitored and guarded the *Rottenführer*'s course. The two *Rotten* flew in a loose line abreast formation, but with the rear *Rotte* echeloned back so that effectively the wingman concept extended by *Rotte* to the whole *Schwarm*, and resulted in a "finger-four" formation.

BOTTOM

In the case of the *Kette*, once airborne, the aircraft would be staggered below and/or behind each other. *Ketten* would fly at 1,000ft intervals. The pilots of JV 44 would also take off in elements of three, as runway widths at Munich-Riem allowed this.

In November it became a part of the First Tactical Air Force, in company with the 320th BG and French B-26 units. The First Tactical Air Force left Corsica and moved to bases in southern France, with the 17th being posted to Rouvres-en-Plaine near Dijon, where it would remain until the end of the war. As the Allied pincers closed on the Third Reich, so the Marauders of the First Tactical Air Force joined in missions with medium bombers of the Ninth Air Force.

By mid-April 1945, JV 44 had been reinforced with the arrival of more experienced pilots – both unit commanders and instructors. These included Oberst Günther Lützow, ringleader of the perceived "mutiny" against Göring. A former *Kommodore* of JG 3, holder of the Knight's Cross with Oak Leaves since October 1941, and only the second fighter pilot to be credited with 100 victories, his last post had been as a regional fighter commander in northern Italy – a position from which he was removed and told to report to Galland. Oberleutnant Franz Stigler came from II./JG 27, with whom he had flown 480 combat missions over North Africa, Italy, and in the defense of the Reich. Credited with shooting down 28 enemy aircraft, he had been slated for jet training with III./EJG 2 and volunteered to join JV 44.

Galland had been developing and refining his unit's tactics, favoring the use of the three-aircraft *Kette* formation over the Luftwaffe's more customary four-aircraft *Schwarm* as used by piston-engined fighter units. Although speed was one of the Me 262's greatest attributes, it also presented pilots with one of their greatest challenges. Decisions regarding an attack against bombers had to be made quickly and often at great distances from the target, as Galland explained:

My pilots were authorized to open fire from 600m. They were also permitted to fire a short burst before that if they noticed that they were being fired upon by the bombers. We also fired our R4M rockets at that range. We often hit two bombers with them in one go. Me 262 pilots could only count on success in attacking formations of heavy bombers if they were able to approach in fairly close formation, and not if they approached at great distances apart. The Kette had to at least remain at one height, a clear-cut allocation of targets had to be made and the whole Kette had to fire simultaneously in order to make the defensive fire from the bombers disperse.

During the afternoon of April 18, 1945 two *Ketten* of Me 262s were scrambled from Riem to respond to what was one of the most wide-ranging, simultaneous USAAF bombing operations so far mounted against targets across central and southern Germany. Units of the Eighth, Fifteenth, Ninth, and Twelfth Air Forces were active, with B-26s from the latter two forces being sent to strike fuel and rail targets around Ingolstadt, Unterhausen, Ulm, and Oldenburg.

Galland chose once again to lead his jets, and selected Neumann and Stigler to fly in his *Kette*, while Steinhoff would lead Krupinski and Leutnant Gottfried Fährmann in the second *Kette* – altogether, four Knight's Cross-holders, and between all six pilots, more than 550 victories.

As the second *Kette* rolled along the strip, reaching 125mph, the port wing of Steinhoff's Me 262 suddenly dropped after his mainwheel struck debris left on the field from the previous day's bombing raid. The jet began to swerve to the left, dangerously close to Krupinski who was behind him. Krupinski hauled his control column back and lifted into the air just in time to avoid a collision, flying over Steinhoff's Me 262, which was now heading irreversibly, and still at speed, towards an embankment at the end of the strip. A second or so later, Krupinski became aware of an explosion which buffeted his aircraft. Neumann was also airborne, but realizing something was very wrong, for an instant looked back, horrified, towards the ground. Steinhoff's aircraft was now an inferno.

Flying through the smoke palling across the field, the five remaining pilots continued with their mission, but it proved a fruitless sortie. When they returned they were ready for the worst, certain Steinhoff had been killed. But he

Oberst Johannes Steinhoff listens to updates on the air situation by telephone link from JV 44's operations room at Feldkirchen while surrounded by several of the unit's pilots. Identifiable, from left to right, are Hauptmann Walter Krupinski, Major Erich Hohagen, Oberst Günther Lützow (in the leather overcoat, reading), Steinhoff (seated), Fahnenjunker-Oberfeldwebel Klaus Neumann (leaning forward, wearing a forage cap), Oberleutnant Klaus Faber and Unteroffizier Eduard Schallmoser (partially obscured, also wearing a forage cap). Faber belonged to a small section of Fw 190D fighters that provided airfield cover for the Me 262s during their vulnerable moments of take-off and landing. (Author's collection)

had escaped, saved by the self-contained metal rear cockpit sub-assembly which held the Me 262's instrument panel and electrical controls, stick and rudder, throttles, seat and battery, and which was intended to break free on impact. Steinhoff was taken to the military hospital at Oberföhring. His war was over, and he would bear the physical scars from the events of that day for the rest of his life.

There was more bad news the following day. Most of the aircraft in a detachment of Me 262s slated for hand-over to JV 44 from III./KG(J) 54 based at Neuburg an der Donau had been destroyed by B-26s after the jets made an interim landing at Erding.

On April 19 JV 44 despatched three Me 262s to intercept Marauders, probably of the 322nd BG, which had just targeted the railway bridge at Donauwörth. Attacking from the rear of the bombers, the German pilots claimed one B-26 shot down, but they actually damaged two. The Marauder crews stated that they had been attacked by "eight to ten Me 262s," which was perhaps an indication of the psychological impact the German jets had on the USAAF bomber crews.

The following day marked Adolf Hitler's 56th birthday. Bombs rained down on Berlin from more than 800 B-17s. The Red Army was only some ten miles from the northeastern outskirts of the city, which now shook under the impact of Russian shelling. In the south, Nuremburg had been captured by the US Army.

In the air, the Ninth Air Force despatched B-26s from the 323rd, 394th, and 397th BGs to bomb the marshaling yard at Memmingen. The 48 Marauders of the 323rd BG flew in three "boxes" comprising eight six-aircraft flights, following a course from their base at Denain-Prouvy, in northern France, across the Rhine and directly into Bavaria. As they headed towards Memmingen, the crews on board the "white tails" had reason to be cautiously optimistic. Operations over the past few weeks against enemy rail yards, oil storage tanks, and ordnance depots had gone reasonably well, with an "acceptable and affordable level of casualties."

At Munich-Riem, having been alerted to the bombers' approach, a formation of five *Ketten* of Me 262s took off between 1030 and 1100 hrs to intercept the B-26s, being guided towards the enemy formation by their ground control at Feldkirchen.

Flying as part of the 323rd BG's 455th BS that day was B-26F-1 42-96256 *UGLY DUCKLING*, which had been borrowed from the 454th BS. At its controls was 1Lt James L. Vining from Louisiana, embarking on his 40th combat mission. Although the 455th had recently been suffering from a shortage of aircraft, the Ninth Air Force had ordered a maximum effort for the attack, requiring that every available machine that could be made to fly was to fly. Vining remembered:

It was a standard, if macabre, jest that a borrowed plane was usually the worst in the lender's inventory. Among the numerous defects gradually discovered in this particular junkyard fugitive, the immediate and most critical was a malfunctioning bomb release!

The 455th's groundcrews worked hard to fix the bomb release, and *UGLY DUCKLING* was able to start its engines some 30 minutes later than scheduled. This meant that the Marauder was the last of the squadron's aircraft to depart. Vining recalled:

We approached the IP [Initial Point] at Kempten in standard boxes, but as we turned, the flights dispersed in order to hit the target by single flights in trail. We were at

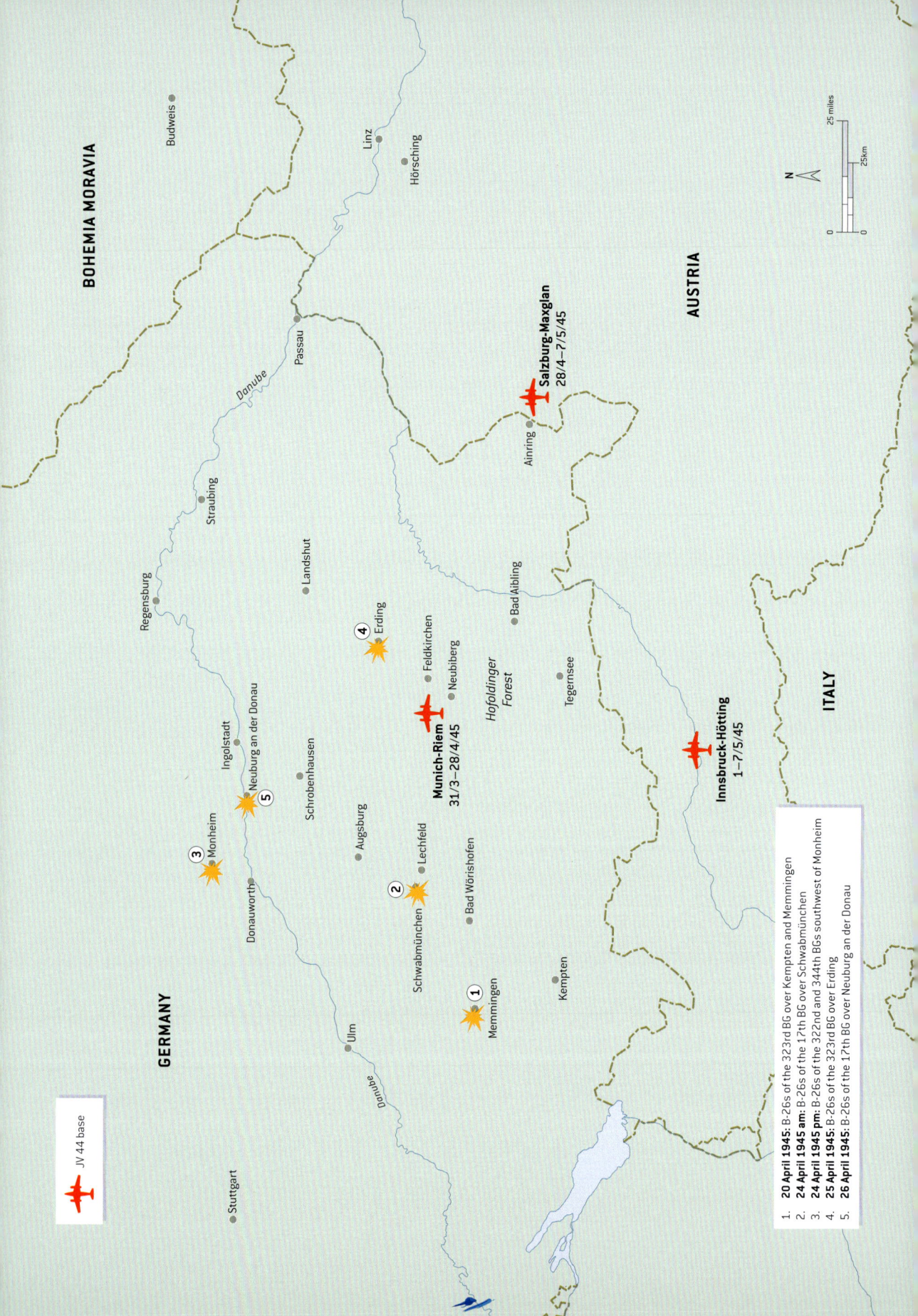

BOHEMIA MORAVIA

GERMANY

AUSTRIA

ITALY

Budweis

Linz

Hörsching

Passau

Danube

Straubing

Landshut

Regensburg

Ainring

Salzburg-Maxglan
28/4–7/5/45

Bad Aibling

Erding

Feldkirchen

Neubiberg

Munich-Riem
31/3–28/4/45

*Hofoldinger
Forest*

Tegernsee

Innsbruck-Hötting
1–7/5/45

Ingolstadt

Neuburg an der Donau

Monheim

Schrobenhausen

Augsburg

Lechfeld

Donauwörth

Bad Wörishofen

Schwabmünchen

Ulm

Danube

Kempten

Memmingen

Stuttgart

JV 44 base

1. **20 April 1945:** B-26s of the 323rd BG over Kempten and Memmingen
2. **24 April 1945 am:** B-26s of the 17th BG over Schwabmünchen
3. **24 April 1945 pm:** B-26s of the 322nd and 344th BGs southwest of Monheim
4. **25 April 1945:** B-26s of the 323rd BG over Erding
5. **26 April 1945:** B-26s of the 17th BG over Neuburg an der Donau

N

25 miles

25km

12,000ft. As we rolled out of the turn onto a four-minute bomb run, I heard from my tail gunner the now dreaded words, *"Fighters coming in from the rear!"*

Flying in the No. 4 position behind the box leader in the 323rd BG formation was a B-26G of the 454th BS piloted by 1Lt Harold C. Day. Ironically, Day's usual aircraft was *UGLY DUCKLING*, but on this mission he was flying a replacement Marauder. Day's radio operator/waist gunner was TSgt Robert M. Radlein:

I was sitting back in my waist position, fat, dumb and happy, not thinking about much of anything really because nothing was happening. The plot unfolded when I glanced out of my window at our No. 6 plane on our left wing and I noticed that its tail gunner was burning out his barrels firing at something, having apparently frozen on the trigger. He never stopped shooting – he just wouldn't let up. I stuck my head out of the left waist window to see what he was shooting at, and just then I saw two of our P-51 escorts flashing across our tail. They too seemed to be burning out their barrels. I figured something must be happening, so I looked out of the right waist window to see what everyone was shooting at, and right then this Me 262 appeared, right up alongside us, "three o'clock level," about 100 yards out, flying, to all practical purposes, in formation with us. Instantly, I charged my gun.

It was just after 1100 hrs, and JV 44's Me 262s were heading west in clear skies in line astern in loose *Ketten* at between 9,800–13,100ft. Sighting the Marauders, Unteroffizier Eduard Schallmoser, flying in the vanguard of the jets, flicked off the safety to his MK 108s. The bombers were still flying in a tight, protective formation. Schallmoser selected a target and pressed the firing button, but he was to be plagued by the same circumstances that took place on April 4 – the MK 108s jammed.

As the other *Ketten* of Me 262s closed in on the B-26s from "six" and "seven o'clock low," the tail gunners opened fire in defense. But the combination of the jets' speed and firepower was devastating. The first bomber to be hit was B-26B 41-31918 *Can't Get Started* of the 454th BS flown by 1Lt Dale E. Sanders. Its port engine began to trail smoke, causing the bomber to fall away from the formation. At his waist gun, TSgt Radlein opened fire:

My gunnery training had taught me to fire short bursts, each of about ten rounds. I did it all automatically. I fired about five bursts at the Me 262 – about 50 rounds in all – and I watched my tracers lag behind his tail, which probably meant I was punching holes in his fuselage. He pulled away and left the scene, but almost immediately another Me 262 pulled up into the same slot. I don't know what they had in their minds, but it was giving me good target practice, so I fired off two

A rearkable air-to-air photograph taken from the waist position of a B-26 of the 323rd BG on April 20, 1945 as an Me 262 of JV 44 passes through the flight of Marauders seen at the base of the photograph and flying below B-26G-25 44-68132 of the 456th BS. The jet is visible as the small light-colored aircraft passing just behind the rearmost B-26 at the right of the flight. Another B-26 in the rear flight, just visible immediately below 44-68132, appears to have been hit and is on fire, possibly as a result of being attacked by the jet. Photo via John Moench. (Robert Forsyth Collection)

bursts at the second Me 262 and then my gun jammed. I cleared the jam in about two or three seconds, but by that time he had gone.

Our top turret gunner, SSgt Edmundo Estrada, started firing. He had just raised his guns straight up and was shooting at an Me 262 passing overhead when he yelled "*I got him! I got him!*" because he saw all kinds of metal and debris come flying past our aircraft. Estrada was convinced he had hit the jet, but unfortunately the pieces of metal he had seen had come not from the German fighter, but from our No. 3 aircraft piloted by Lt Sanders. I looked out of my left waist window at Sanders' plane as it started to drop away, and was able to see the entire radio compartment. The fighter attack had stripped away all the metal from the top of the wing and the compartments for the radio man and navigator – I guess from just aft of the windows in the pilot's compartment. One engine was also gone. As I watched Sanders' bomber fall out of formation, I reached over to snap on my chest pack 'chute – things were warming up pretty fast.

From the cockpit of *UGLY DUCKLING*, 1Lt James Vining watched the jets streak past above him so close to the neighboring Marauders that they only narrowly avoided their tail fins and propellers:

A third jet zoomed in, barely clearing No. 4, and I instantly knew that he could not go over No. 1. There seemed to be no room for him to go under, so I braced myself for a horrible mid-air collision, but he managed to nose down just enough to go under the right wing, and in the process run his rudder through the right propeller, slicing about half the jet's rudder off.

In his Me 262 "White 11," Schallmoser glanced down at his control column in frustration when his guns jammed. When he looked back up, it was just too late to avoid striking the propeller blades of B-26G 44-68109 flown by 1Lt James M. Hansen of the 455th BS. Upon impact, the Me 262 rolled over and nosed down through the enemy formation, with pieces of the jet's own debris falling behind it. However, Hansen was able to control his aircraft, even keeping the right-hand engine running, despite the blades having been evenly bent six inches from their tips, and he returned successfully to base.

Schallmoser recounted:

Basically, I turned too late and rammed the Marauder, which then fell away. Meanwhile, I knew my "White 11" was a complete loss, and with my last reserves of strength I was able to escape the aircraft by parachute.

On April 20, 1945, B-26s from three bomb groups of the Ninth Air Force were sent out to target marshaling yard at Memmingen. JV 44 put up a relatively large force of Me 262s to intercept them, and in the ensuing combat B-26B-30 41-31918 *Can't Get Started* of the 454th BS/323rd BG was shot down. The bomber's crew, led by 1Lt Dale E. Sanders, parachuted into captivity. (USAF)

Remarkably good fortune would remain with Schallmoser, for having bailed out of his aircraft, he came down in his mother's garden in the small town of Lenzfried-im-Allgau. Folding up his parachute and suffering from a painful blow to one of his knees from when he left his aircraft, he limped into the family home, where his bewildered mother fed him with a plate of pancakes.

Meanwhile, in Me 262 "White 15" Unteroffizier Johann-Karl Müller, a former ground-attack pilot who joined JV 44 from II./SG 10, having flown Fw 190s over the Mediterranean, the USSR, and the Western Front, made contact with the Marauders at 9,800ft over Kempten. Each wing of his jet was loaded with a battery of 12 55mm R4M air-to-air rockets, and the next few seconds would be testimony to the effectiveness of this new aerial weapon. Müller depressed the firing switch and the rockets hissed away from their racks.

Aboard *UGLY DUCKLING*, 1Lt Vining spotted an Me 262 closing in:

B-26G-25 44-68109 of the 455th BS/323rd BG, flown by 1Lt James M. Hansen, was lucky to make it back to its base at Denain-Prouvy, in France, following the JV 44 attack on April 20, 1945. The effects of Unteroffizier Eduard Schallmoser's close pass just beneath the Marauder's starboard engine are clearly visible on the propeller tips. Photo via John Moench. (Robert Forsyth Collection)

I turned my attention back to my position, tucking my wing closer to No. 4, and at that instant a terrific blast went off below my knees and the plane rolled to the right. Sensing that my right leg was gone, I looked toward my co-pilot, and while ordering him to take his controls, I noted that the right engine was at idle speed. So, in one swift arcing motion with my right hand, I hit the feathering button, moved to the overhead rudder trim crank and trimmed the plane for single engine operation, and, just as rapidly, pressed the intercom button to order the bombardier to jettison the two tons of bombs. We were losing altitude at 2,000ft per minute, which slowed to 1,000ft per minute with the load gone.

As Vining's B-26 fell away from its formation, the relatively inexperienced co-pilot took control of the aircraft and the radio operator/navigator applied a tourniquet to Vining's shattered leg, together with some morphine. The main artery had been spraying blood around the cockpit and the foot was "dangling by a shred of skin." Meanwhile, the lone "straggler" began to attract more attacks from the jets, which attempted to finish

A battery of 12 55mm R4M *Orkan* air-to-air rockets attached to their wooden launch rack as fitted to the underside of the starboard wing of an Me 262A-1a of JG 7. The same weapon was used to devastating effect by JV 44 against B-26 Marauders over southern Germany in April 1945. (EN Archive)

it off. Miraculously, despite the substantial damage inflicted by one of Müller's R4Ms, the Marauder remained airborne. Even with a further attack by Me 262s of I./KG(J) 54, it managed to return to friendly territory, where the bomber crash-landed on an abandoned airfield close to the French border.

JV 44's attack on the 323rd BG had resulted in the loss of three B-26s and one entire crew, with seven more Marauders damaged. No German pilots were reported lost, but Schallmoser's aircraft was destroyed and it is likely several others had been damaged during the engagement.

During the morning of April 20, 1945 the Ninth Air Force despatched B-26s from three bomb groups to attack the marshaling yard at Memmingen, in Bavaria. Some 48 Marauders involved in the mission came from the 323rd BG based at Prouvy, in France. As the bombers crossed the Rhine, at Munich-Riem JV 44 scrambled around 15 Me 262s in formations of three-aircraft *Ketten* to engage. The jets intercepted the B-26s shortly after 1100 hrs due south of Memmingen. Approaching from behind the American formation, one *Kette*, including the R4M rocket-armed Me 262 "White 15" flown by Unteroffizier Karl-Heinz Müller, launched an attack on a flight of B-26s from the 323rd BG's 455th BS just as it was about to make its bomb-run. As Müller and his two comrades fired their salvos of rockets into the formation, one R4M struck B-26F-1 42-96256, *UGLY DUCKLING*, flown by 1Lt James L. Vining. The effect of the R4M was devastating, the rocket striking the Marauder just below the cockpit and shooting upwards through the aircraft before exiting the upper fuselage aft of the cockpit. The right engine failed as a result of the strike and the Marauder fell away to the right as the three Me 262s swept through the flight. It was only down to the swift emergency action taken by Vining, in combination with his flying skills, that saved all bar one of his crew. Miraculously despite suffering severe injuries, further attacks by Me 262s and the loss of an engine, Vining was able fly his aircraft back to friendly territory and crash-land.

The 323rd BG returned in the afternoon to bomb the rail yard at Nordlingen, and although an Me 262 did appear, it did not attack the bombers.

JV 44 continued to engage the "mediums" over the coming days. On April 24, the 17th BG was one of several groups to be deployed by the First Tactical Air Force early in the morning against a range of targets in southern Germany. Ten B-26s flying from Rouvres-en-Plaine, escorted by Mustangs, attempted to bomb an ordnance depot at Schwabmünchen, to the south of Augsburg, but their efforts were frustrated by inclement weather and technical problems. Undeterred, the 17th returned for a third run against the target, and this time it ran into trouble.

Only around 60 miles from Riem, the Me 262s were able to reach the bombers quickly. At 0950 hrs, JV 44 sent up a formation of 11 jets led by Oberst Lützow, with each aircraft carrying batteries of R4M rockets. Just 12 minutes later, the lead *Kette* of Me 262s swept towards the three Marauders forming the three-aircraft "window" or "chaff" flight tasked with blotting enemy radar screens. They flew apart from the other aircraft when conducting this vital mission. At precisely 1002 hrs, just as the flight was leaving the target to re-join the main formation, the three Me 262s hit the Marauders from above and behind in line astern, closing in to 2,700ft before they fired their R4Ms in salvos. It was the first time the crews of the 17th had experienced a jet attack, as Sgt Warren E. Young, an engineer/gunner aboard a B-26 of the 37th BS, remembered:

April 24th, we were attacked by jets for the first time. The first time I saw an Me 262, he was coming straight for us from "five o'clock high." I opened fire and in a matter of seconds he was overhead. I pushed the red high-speed button on my turret to turn it so that I could fire on him again as he was flying away, but before the turret had completed its 180-degree turn, the jet had gone. As I looked over the side of our plane, I saw a wing break off one of our bombers and then the plane went into a spin.

Sgt Young and his fellow crewmen watched in horror as an R4M speared into the No. 1 aircraft of the "window" flight, B-26C 42-107729 *STUD DUCK* of the 34th BS. Piloted by 1Lt Fred J. Harms, the Marauder had been with the 17th BG since June 1944 and had flown a string of nearly ten perfect missions as a flight leader with a different crew. Armorer/gunner SSgt Hal S. Brink had called out a warning of enemy fighters, but it was too late. The B-26 took a direct hit to its vertical stabilizer, causing the bomber to roll to the right, narrowly missing the No. 2 aircraft. The Marauder's wing was observed to be badly damaged, as was the waist position and aft bomb-bay area, and moments later it went into a spin, disappearing into clouds with its wheels down and bomb-bay doors open.

Aboard *STUD DUCK*, the impact and blast caused by the R4M had been so great that it forced engineer/gunner SSgt Edward F. Truver out of the aircraft. As he later recounted:

Right after we started shooting at the enemy planes there was an explosion which blew me out of my gun position and out of the plane. I happened to have my parachute on, so I was able to come down safely. Upon reaching the ground, I landed just a short distance from our burning plane. I didn't see any other 'chutes while I was coming down.

The Germans who took me prisoner told me that I was the only one who got out of the plane.

STUD DUCK crashed around eight miles from Babenhausen. An R4M accounted for at least one other B-26B of the 34th BS, with 42-95987 *YO-YO CHAMP*, flown by 1Lt Leigh Slates, going down with the loss of its entire six-man crew. Among several German claims for this mission, Feldwebel Otto Kammerdiener, flying "White 3," was credited with one bomber confirmed shot down. JV 44 also reported the loss of an unidentified *oberfähnrich*.

During the afternoon a force of 74 B-26s from the 322nd and 344th BGs based in Belgium headed for Schrobenhausen, some 30 miles north of Munich, where they were to bomb an oil storage depot which was intended to supply fuel to German forces pulling back into the Alpine "Redoubt" area of southern Germany and Austria. The B-26s would be accompanied by 41 A-20 Havocs from the 410th BG.

Once more, Oberst Lützow was airborne, leading a formation of six Me 262s up from Riem in cloudy skies, although two of the jets were forced to turn back because of engine problems. Aside from Lützow, two of the remaining aircraft were flown by Krupinski and Neumann. The fighters of Lützow and Neumann were carrying R4M rockets.

The Havocs struggled to find the target in the cloud as a result of their pathfinder aircraft suffering from equipment failure, and with visual bombing impossible because of the murky skies, the formation had to abort and turn back for home. The B-26s pressed on, flying in three "boxes" about 20 minutes apart. Their pathfinders fared better than those assigned to guide the A-20s, and as they approached the target their crews armed their bombs. As they did so, the four Me 262s from JV 44 were coming up from the south at speed, across the Swabian Jura, to intercept. At 1527 hrs, just before the last element of bombers from the 344th BG was about to make its bomb-run, the jets broke out from the clouds at 23,000ft, diving to around 11,000ft to attack the Marauders' "window" flight southeast of Monheim, splitting up to make two attacks from "six o'clock level" and "two o'clock high."

The Marauder gunners immediately opened fire, but the jets flashed past and disappeared back into the clouds. 2Lt William P. Morton was piloting a B-26 of the 494th BS/344th BG, flying in the No. 6 position of the group's third flight:

I only recall the intercom conversation about some strange-looking fighters shooting cannon at us. According to my gunners, they were well

The mangled remains of B-26F-1 42-96256 *UGLY DUCKLING* of the 454th BS/323rd BG after its crash-landing close to the French border on April 20, 1945. Photo via James Vining. (Robert Forsyth Collection)

The crew of Omaha-built B-26C-45 42-107729 *STUD DUCK* pose by their aircraft, which was on the strength of the 34th BS/17th BG from early June 1944. It was hit by an R4M fired by an Me 262 of JV 44 on April 24, 1945, the force generated by the rocket exploding blowing engineer/gunner SSgt Edward F. Truver out of the aircraft. He survived, but the rest of the crew perished when the bomber crashed eight miles from Babenhausen. Photo via Ronnie Macklin. (Robert Forsyth Collection)

B-26B-50 42-95987 *YO-YO CHAMP* flew more than 100 missions with the 497th BS/344th BG prior to being transferred to the 34th BS/17th BG. The veteran bomber had been with the latter unit less than a month when it became the second 17th BG Marauder to be shot down over Schwabmünchen by Me 262s of JV 44 on April 24, 1945. (USAF)

out of range of our guns. I then caught a glimpse of this object out of my left eye, and it was moving like a bat out of Hell.

Sgt Jonny Quong was Morton's engineer/top turret gunner:

I saw what seemed at first to be a twin-engine B-26 straggler at long distance approaching at "six o'clock." As it kept approaching, all the gunners saw it. It kept coming and then dived and broke off to the left. When it turned, I could tell it was not a B-26, but a smaller plane going like a bat out of Hell. All the gunners started talking excitedly. "What the Hell was that?" We were so excited that our pilot had to tell us to keep quiet.

Neumann immediately fired his rockets and thought he observed two Marauders break out of formation, while Krupinski saw another B-26 trailing black smoke from its port engine but managing to remain with the group. However, moments after they made their attack, the jets were forced to break up because P-47D Thunderbolts of the 365th FG, assigned as escort that day, dived past the bombers in pursuit.

2Lt James L. Stalter, flying B-26G 43-34181 *Lak-a-Nookie* of the 344th BG, remembered:

We were heading for home when I heard our Group Leader call the leader of our P-47 escort, stating, "*We have visitors.*" The fighter leader's response still sticks in my mind. In a very, very slow southern Texas drawl, he responded, "*Okay. We'll be right down.*" One Me 262 passed on our right and at our level at a very high rate of speed and in level flight. He was followed by a P-47 in close pursuit. While still within visual range, the Me 262 rolled over and did a split-S down into the cloud layer. The P-47 followed with the same maneuver and disappeared from my view.

B-26G 43-34293 of the 494th BS was being flown by 2Lt Doug R. Zimmerman. The radio operator/gunner aboard the aircraft was Sgt Don E. Sinclair on his 15th bombing mission. He was just beginning to relax after the Marauder had dropped its bombs, Zimmerman having started to turn back to base, when:

We were suddenly attacked by Me 262 jets that came up firing through our flight. I heard their shells exploding near our left engine. Our top turret gunner, Sgt Norman Chapman, fired at one as it passed by. The tail gunner, Sgt Glenn L. Tawney, saw one as it banked away, and he would have had the perfect shot as the jet had its belly and the underside of its wings exposed. In the instant Glenn saw the jet, the two engine pods resembled the engines on a B-26, and he thought that it was one of our planes. When he realized it was an Me 262, it was gone and it was too late to fire at it.

One of the jets hung between our plane and the No. 6 in our flight. As I aimed my gun, I could see our No. 6 in my sights, and I didn't fire for fear of hitting the B-26. But

B-26 Marauder basic flight formations

Differing formation structures were adopted by B-26s dependent on mission type, as laid out in the December 1944 pilot training manual.

The flight was a three-aircraft element and could be flown as either a "vee," "echelon" or "stagger." Three vee elements would form a larger vee-shaped, nine-aircraft, squadron-sized "box" formation of identical structure and shape as the three-aircraft vee, with the lead three-aircraft vee flying slightly lower. Alternatively, a squadron could fly its three vees in a "Javelin Down" line astern formation, trailing downwards.

Similarly, squadrons could be flown "staggered," with a lead vee followed by another vee behind, below and to the left in the direction of flight, while the rearmost vee would be behind, to the right and higher. An echeloned back formation, with three vees stepped upwards, diagonally line astern from left to right, could also be used.

Two "boxes" would form a group-sized formation of 27 aircraft. This would be flown staggered, comprised of three nine-aircraft squadrons formed of three vees flying line astern trailing downwards.

Finally, a group could also fly as a "diamond" with four six-aircraft elements, each of two vees, with a lead element flanked at left low and right high, and a rear element of Marauders trailing lower than the rest of the formation.

Two or more groups would make a "bomber formation".

Each of these combinations was intended to provide "flexibility, compactness and firepower."

Flight Vee

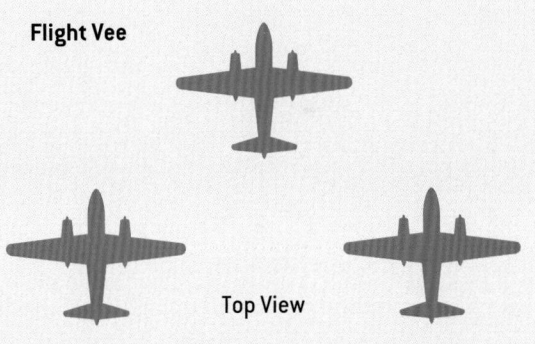

Top View

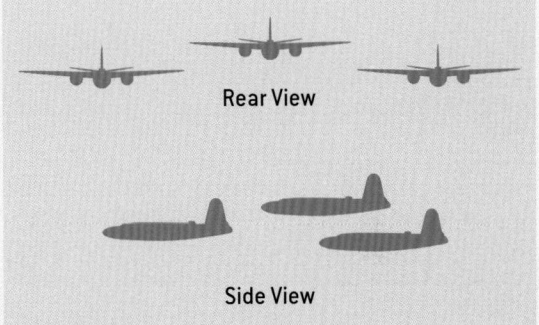

Rear View

Side View

Flight Echelon

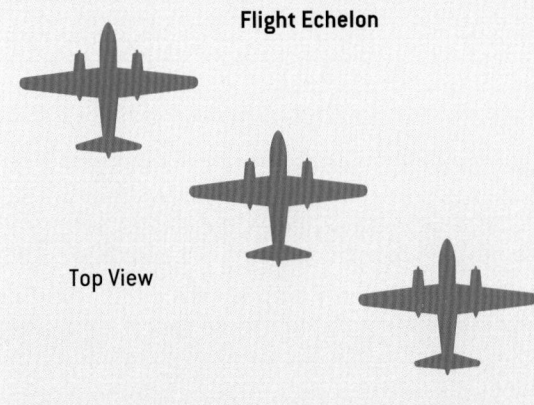

Top View

Flight Stagger

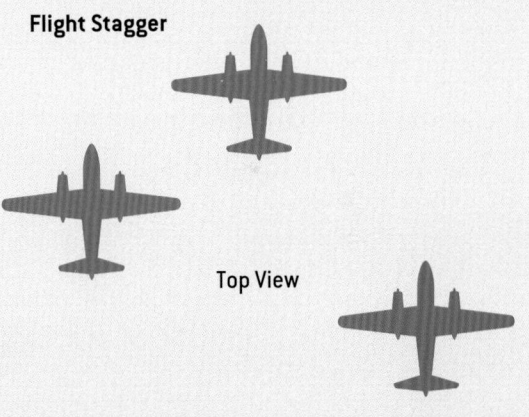

Top View

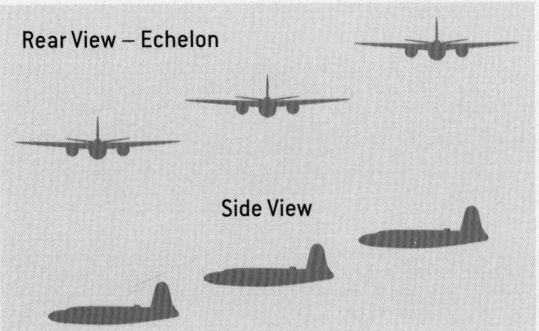

Rear View – Echelon

Side View

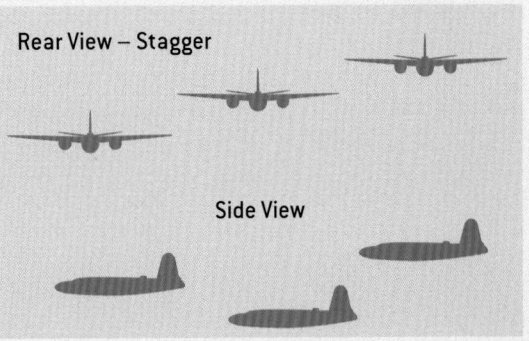

Rear View – Stagger

Side View

I could see the German pilot's face very clearly as he was that close. He was probably there for only a few seconds, but at the time it seemed a lot longer. In an instant he was gone.

The German pilots now attempted to regroup and return as quickly as possible to Riem, aware that they were outnumbered by the P-47s. The Me 262s made a wide left turn homeward in loose formation, with Lützow's aircraft positioned furthest to the south. At this stage Lützow's comrades were unaware that radio contact with him had been lost, but Krupinski observed his jet suddenly turn further to the south away from the other Me 262s and towards the mountains. Moments later Krupinski saw an explosion in the air about 12 miles away. He tried to raise Lützow by radio, but to no avail.

Low on fuel, the three remaining Me 262s landed back at Riem and their pilots made three probable claims over B-26s, although the Americans reported no aircraft missing. Oberst Günther Lützow did not return, and it is believed that his Me 262 had crashed into some waste ground in the town of Donauwörth, between Ulm and Ingolstadt, having been fatally damaged in the attack by P-47s of the 365th FG. For the personnel of JV 44, his loss was a severe blow.

JV 44 was active again on the afternoon of April 25. The unit prepared 13 Me 262s in two formations, one to carry out free-ranging patrols against enemy fighters, the other to take on B-26s heading to Erding airfield and a neighboring ammunition dump. Problems affected both operations early on, with five jets being forced to return after take-off due to technical problems, while two more were recalled for unspecified reasons. Of those machines which continued, three encountered P-47s over Augsburg in an engagement without result or loss to either side, while the other three took on bombers between Landshut and Erding.

One of these latter Me 262s was an experimental A-1a/U4 with a long-barreled Mauser 50mm MK 214 cannon installed in its nose. Who was actually flying this aircraft remains unclear, but what is known is that it engaged B-26s of the 323rd and 344th BGs. Just before 1750 hrs a single Me 262 was spotted by crews of the 323rd BG shadowing their formation, way out to the right, just after they had turned away from the target. It is probable that this was the Me 262A-1a/U4. The jet circled around the third box of Marauders to make attacks from both behind and directly in front, closing in to about 500 yards, but without opening fire, before diving away to the right.

Capt John O. Moench was flying as Group Lead with the 323rd BG, and he remembered:

Suddenly the intercom came to life with the call-out of fighters taking off from Erding Airdrome below. Almost instantly someone called out a fighter at "one o'clock." I looked up, and well out in front of us, swinging around for what looked like a frontal attack, was an Me 262. As the enemy pilot turned, the 50mm cannon sticking out of the nose of the Me 262 had the appearance of a giant telephone pole. Seconds later, the Me 262 had passed well over the formation without firing a shot and well out of range of our .50s. Then we spotted him swinging around in a wide circle seemingly to get into position to make another frontal pass. Again, he remained out of firing range and disappeared.

Almost instantly, there was a call from the tail gunner that an Me 262 was off the rear. Crossing from the right, the jet swung around and came back from the left. Nineteen of the gunners opened up on the Me 262 at maximum range and, apparently discouraged by the barrage of fire from the Marauders, the pilot broke off.

There was some consolation for JV 44, however, when Unteroffizier Franz Köster, newly arrived from JG 7, shot down a P-51 and a P-38.

The combat attrition grinding at JV 44's small number of operational pilots was about to reach existential levels. At 1120 hrs on April 26, Galland led a force of 12 of the unit's 43 available

B-26 Marauders of the 17th BG fly in close formation as they approach their target. This was the view an Me 262 pilot of JV 44 would have had during an attack mounted from the rear and below. Photo via Ronnie Macklin. (Robert Forsyth Collection)

Me 262s to engage B-26s of the 17th BG out to bomb the recently evacuated jet base at Lechfeld and the ammunition dump at Schrobenhausen. They were part of a larger force from the USAAF's 42nd BW, together with French Marauders. All the jets were armed with R4Ms, but as they climbed, one aircraft was forced to turn back because of an engine problem.

Thirty minutes later, over Neuburg, the German pilots spotted around 60 Marauders escorted by a similar number of P-47s. The "mediums" had just aborted their bombing run due to the increasingly heavy cloud when JV 44's Me 262s closed in from head-on and then flashed over the bomber formation, to circle around in a dive for an attack from below. Flying as Galland's wingman, Unteroffizier Schallmoser, freshly out of hospital the day before, and with a knee injury still troubling him, fired his rockets and watched as a B-26 "blew apart in the air."

Flying a little above Schallmoser, Galland armed his Me 262's four MK 108s and flicked off the safety to the R4Ms. Already, the Marauder tail gunners had opened fire at the approaching jets, and as he closed in, Galland selected as his target the outermost and rearmost B-26 of the first box.

Meanwhile, one of the gunners firing at the Germans was SSgt Albert Linz aboard B-26B 42-95771 *MY GAL SAL* of the 37th BS/17th BG:

Assuming that Galland was leading the three jets which came in on us, the wingman on his left selected us for a target and hit our left engine. Galland and his two buddies passed directly beneath us, about 300–400ft away, heading to the rear of our formation. This was my first sight of a jet plane, and they sure looked strange with no propellers.

Galland depressed his rocket firing switch but nothing happened. In the speed of his approach – just a matter of seconds – he had omitted to flick off the second safety switch for the rockets, probably as a result of being distracted by the return fire. He fired a burst from his cannon at a B-26, which erupted into flames, before passing

ENGAGING THE ENEMY

JV 44 is known to have deployed the 55mm R4M *Orkan* air-to-air rocket against formations of B-26 Marauders. However, it seems the weapon was used only by the unit's more experienced pilots, and the R4M was subject to dwindling availability. Although the rocket demanded skill in piloting and targeting, its effect could be deadly. Here, a pilot of JV 44 approaches the rear of a tight Marauder formation and fires his battery of R4Ms from as close to the bombers as he can get before diving below them.

The R4M was an unrotated, rail- or tube-launched, single venturi, solid fuel propelled, multi-fin stabilized missile, with the warhead contained in an exceptionally thin one-millimeter sheet steel case enclosed in two pressed steel sections welded together and holding the Hexogen high-explosive charge. The missile bore a high charge weight to case weight ratio.

Batteries, to a maximum of 12 rockets, were launched from wooden underwing racks positioned outside of the engines. The R4M was intended primarily as an anti-bomber weapon, designed to create panic within a formation and to force it to scatter. The rockets' deployment against fighters was much rarer, though not unknown.

through the center of the American formation, from where he fired at another bomber.

1Lt John W. Sorrelle was piloting a Marauder of the 432nd BS at 12,000ft, flying as deputy lead in the No. 4 position and "tucked in tightly under the tail turret of the flight leader":

My tail gunner, TSgt Cleo E. Wills, broke radio silence on the interphone. "*Bandits coming out of the clouds at 'six o'clock low', climbing and closing fast. They look like 262s.*" I could feel my control column shuddering slightly as he began firing his twin .50-cal machine guns. "*I got him! I got him!*" Wills shouted over the intercom. Then the left wingman at my "ten o'clock" position exploded and was gone.

Around Galland, the waist gunners began to open fire. He heard the thud of enemy shells striking his aircraft and the Messerschmitt started to trail smoke. Galland, nevertheless, remained inquisitive about the fate of the second B-26, and as he left the bombers, he banked his aircraft around to observe.

Manning the waist gun in the lead ship of the 34th BS was TSgt Henry Dietz, a former weapons instructor:

Our experience with the tail guns on the B-26 was that they repeatedly malfunctioned due to the underpowered motor feeding the ammunition belt. The waist guns were gravity fed, which meant you could empty a belt of ammunition without a problem. From the waist position I could see all mechanical parts of the aircraft. I had never seen a jet before. Galland slowed down to the speed of the B-26 to count the take, before coming back to observe and take score. I thought, "*Dummy.*" He was flying low, right into the sights of my machine gun. I shot a burst. Nothing happened. A little higher, a little lower, I just kept shooting.

It is still unclear which Marauder was Galland's second victim, but *MY GAL SAL* had been hit in the port engine and was trailing black smoke. 'As we fell out of formation,' SSgt Albert Linz recalled, 'the last thing I saw was our No. 5 plane completely enveloped in flames.'

For 1Lt John Sorrelle and his crew, the JV 44 attack had inflicted significant damage on their aircraft:

My plane did a violent wingover to the left and dove straight for the ground. Thinking I'd lost the No. 1 engine, I idled both throttles to regain control. The aircraft was still rolling to the left. I advanced the throttles. Both engines were good. I started cranking in the right rudder trim. Ordinarily, it took one to two degrees to counter take-off torque and no more than five or six after losing an engine. I needed 11.5 degrees to straighten the plane out. The limit is 15. Airspeed redline for the B-26 is 353mph. We were nearly

B-26B-45 42-95771 *MY GAL SAL* of the 37th BS/17th BG was photographed on April 26, 1945 shortly after crash-landing at Luneville with power from only one engine after being targeted by Me 262s of JV 44. The Marauder, which had joined the 17th BG at Villacidro, on Sardinia, in February 1944, was declared a write-off as a result of the Me 262 attack. Photo via Ronnie Macklin. (Robert Forsyth Collection)

TSgt Henry Dietz of the 34th BS/17th BG at the waist gun position in a B-26 Marauder. Of the JV 44 attack led by Galland on April 26, 1945, he recalled, "He [Galland] was flying low, right into the sights of my machine gun. I shot a burst. Nothing happened. A little higher, a little lower, I just kept shooting." Photo via Henry Dietz. (Robert Forsyth Collection)

past it. The ground was coming up fast. Fearing wing failure, I began gingerly using the elevator trim tab. The airspeed bled off as the nose crept up. We were just above the treetops. The jets were gone and our squadronmates were barely visible in the distance. We used emergency power to re-join the formation.

Over the course of five firing passes, the Me 262s had inflicted carnage on the bomber formation, attacking from a bewildering number of angles and directions, which taxed the American gunners' skills to their limits. Any cohesion within the 17th BG's formation was lost, and only one of the group's four squadrons survived without loss – and this despite the presence of four groups of fighter escort. Shortly after midday, P-47Ds of the 27th and 50th FGs came to the aid of the bombers, diving down from a higher altitude and firing their machine guns as they gave chase to the now quickly dispersing jets. The Thunderbolts would prove to be Galland's nemesis. He wrote:

A hail of fire enveloped me. A sharp rap hit my right knee, the instrument panel with its indispensable instruments was shattered, the right engine was also hit – its metal covering worked loose in the wind and was partly carried away – and now the left engine was hit. I could hardly hold her in the air.

One-by-one, the jets returned home, having claimed five B-26s, including one kill each for Unteroffizier Schallmoser and Feldwebel Kammerdiener. JV 44 had lost two pilots, although one of them had managed to bail out. Kammerdiener's jet had been hit in the right-hand engine, setting it on fire – his subsequent landing at Riem proved difficult on the remaining, functioning engine. Following in Kammerdiener at around 1230 hrs was a shaken Galland. Both his engines had been hit in the fighter attack and metal fragments had been sucked into the port-side Jumo's manifold. Shells had also entered the Me 262's cockpit from the rear, and, as a result, Galland had to contend with metal splinters which had embedded themselves in his knee and controls that no longer functioned. He flew over the Autobahn on his approach to Riem:

Having regained my self-confidence, I gave the customary wing wobble and started banking to come in. It was remarkably quiet and dead below. One engine did not react at all to the throttle, and as I could not reduce it, I had to cut both engines just before the edge of the airfield. A long trail of smoke drifted behind me.

The Me 262 bumped to a halt with a flat tire as Galland threw open the canopy and clambered out awkwardly, just as Allied fighter-bombers began a strafing run over Riem. His flying days were over, and those of his unit would not last much longer.

STATISTICS AND ANALYSIS

The closing months of World War II heralded the dawn of a new era in air combat in which a small number of next-generation Me 262 jet- and Me 163 rocket-powered interceptors engaged a much larger Allied "fleet" of heavy and medium bombers, along with their fighter escort. It is not a generalization to say that, essentially,

The 9th Bombardment Division flew its final mission on May 3, 1945, although aside from eight B-26s of the 1st Pathfinder Squadron (Provisional), this was an A-26 Invader operation. Nevertheless, the B-26 probably played a greater role in the tactical bombing of Europe than the A-20 Havoc. Bombers of the Ninth Air Force flew 9,409 sorties, losing 44 of their number in the process. Photo via Jerry Scutts. (Robert Forsyth Collection)

As the US Army pushed deeper into southern Germany in the closing weeks of the war, so it discovered and uncovered the Third Reich's emergency jet aircraft manufacturing infrastructure. Here, a GI stops to inspect abandoned Me 262s in one of several "*Waldwerke*" ("forest factories") in the region. (EN Archive)

overwhelming Allied air power defeated the more advanced and superior aeronautical technology of the Third Reich.

It is believed that Nazi Germany built a little over 1,400 Me 262 production series aircraft, although the historical record is varied and contradictory, so the true total may never be known. It is also believed that around 300 of all variants were delivered to operational units, although how many went into action is again unknown.

Some 5,266 B-26s – all variants – were built between 1940–44. Of this total, 1,883 were B-models, 300 were F-models and 893 were G-models. Deliveries (all variants) were 4,450 to the USAAF, 272 to the US Navy, and 544 to the RAF.

Numbers are very vague, but from what scant records survive, along with the few personal accounts from the unit's pilots, it can be assumed that between early April and 7 May 1945, JV 44 claimed between 15 and 20 Marauders shot down. The actual number totally lost is probably less than ten. B-26 gunners claimed several Me 262s either shot down or damaged. JV 44 probably lost, literally, one or two to defensive fire, although there is no doubt several suffered varying degrees of damage.

AFTERMATH

Generalleutnant Adolf Galland was hospitalized following the wounds he had incurred in the attack on his Me 262 by P-47s near Schrobenhausen on April 26, 1945. From his hospital bed, for a brief time, he endeavored to retain command over his unit, assisted by nightfighter ace Major Wilhelm Herget as his "Adjutant for Special Duties," but it proved impractical. Day-to-day operational command of JV 44 passed to the former *Kommandeur* of III./EJG 2, Oberstleutnant Heinz Bär (see Chapter 6), who had arrived at Munich-Riem from Lechfeld a few days before.

At the eleventh hour, a small band of stellar names had drifted into JV 44, including Germany's second highest-scoring fighter pilot, Major Gerhard Barkhorn, who had joined the unit in mid-April, but he was injured before he could commence operational flying.

However, the war was in its final days. Galland ordered JV 44 to evacuate Riem on April 28. The unit would move to Salzburg as an interim measure, and use specially prepared and camouflaged dispersal facilities off the Munich-Salzburg Autobahn in the Hofoldinger Forest and temporary landing strips along the Autobahn itself, which were to be available for operations within two days. The ultimate destination for the unit was to be Innsbruck, to where JV 44 would also send all Me 262s that had been undergoing repair and maintenance at Riem.

Galland's main aim, however, was to ensure that the Me 262s did not fall into the hands of the Red Army. After using Herget to conduct covert negotiations with local US Army units on his behalf,

Stunning *Faith – PRELUDE TO VICTORY* artwork adorned B-26B-50 42-96028, which belonged to the 584th BS/394th BG. It was flown by Capt J. R. Tosi. Photo via John Moench. (Robert Forsyth Collection)

A panoramic view of the damaged airport at Munich-Riem as photographed by the 13th Photographic Reconnaissance Squadron of the 7th Photographic Reconnaissance Group on June 7, 1945. At least four aircraft – an Me 262, two Fw 190Ds, and an Si 204 – belonging to JV 44 can be seen abandoned close to the compass swinging base in front of the bombed-out airport buildings. (Robert Forsyth Collection)

this was accomplished as Allied forces advanced deeper into Austria and Galland surrendered formally to the Americans on May 5, 1945.

With the war won, that same year in the United States, the order was given to terminate B-26 Marauder production at both Middle River and Omaha. As a result, the Glenn Martin company made significant lay-offs across its workforce, although a sufficient number remained employed to work on new projects, including the modification of 1,200 Douglas C-54 Skymasters into commercial DC-4 configuration for airline use.

In the late fall of 1945, 500 Marauders used in the ETO were ferried to a sprawling assembly center at Landsberg am Lech, less than 60 miles from Munich-Riem. Here, the "mediums" were stripped of their engines, radio equipment, and other items deemed to be of value. The scrapping teams concluded that the most efficient and economical way to break up what remained of a B-26 was to fix packs of explosives to the wing roots of each aircraft in order to blow the wings off. More explosives were then attached to the fuselages and they too were blown apart, before US Army bulldozers pushed the wrecks into enormous piles of scrap metal. This metal was later recycled for use within a new, post-war German aluminum industry.

FURTHER READING

In addition to interviews and personal correspondence between the author and former aircrew on both sides, as well as the study of many documents from archives and private collections, the following is a selection of key published works and websites consulted during the writing of this book.

BOOKS/PERIODICALS

Austin, Lambert D. (Ed.), *344th Bomb Group (M) 'Silver Streaks' – History & Remembrances World War II* (Southern Heritage Press, 1996)

Boehme, Manfred, *JG 7 – The World's First Jet Fighter Unit 1944/1945* (Schiffer Military History, 1992)

Brady, Paul M., *Marauder vs Stormbird! A date with fate in the skies over Amberg* (Air Classics, August 1995)

Earl, O. K., *The Thunderbird Goes to War – A Diary of the 34th Bombardment Squadron in World War II* (Braun-Brumfield Inc, 1991)

Felkin, S. D., Gp Capt, *The Me 262 as a Combat Aircraft, ADI(K) Report No. 323/1945* (June 4, 1945)

Forsyth, Robert, *JV 44 – The Galland Circus* (Classic Publications, 1996)

Forsyth, Robert, *Jagdwaffe – Defending the Reich 1943–1944* (Classic Publications, 2004)

Forsyth, Robert, *Jagdwaffe – Defending the Reich 1944–1945* (Classic Publications, 2005)

Forsyth, Robert, *Osprey Elite Units 27 – Jagdverband 44: Squadron of Experten* (Osprey Publishing, 2008)

Forsyth, Robert, with Scutts, Jerry, *Battle over Bavaria – The B-26 Marauder versus the German Jets* (Classic Publications, 1999)

Freeman, Roger A., *Mighty Eighth War Manual* (Janes, 1984)

Galland, Adolf, *The First and The Last* (Methuen, 1955)

Hammel, Eric, *The Road to Big Week – The Struggle for Daylight Air Supremacy over Western Europe July 1942– February 1944* (Pacifica Military History, 2009)

Havener, J. K., *The Martin B-26 Marauder* (TAB/Aero Books, 1988)

Moench, Maj Gen John O., *Marauder Men – An Account of the Martin B-26 Marauder* (Malia Enterprises Inc., 1989)

Rust, Kenn C., *The 9th Air Force in World War II* (Aero Publishers Inc, 1967)

Rust, Kenn C., *Twelfth Air Force Story* (Historical Aviation Album, 1975)

Scutts, Jerry, *Osprey Combat Aircraft 2 – B-26 Marauder Units of the Eighth and Ninth Air Forces* (Osprey Publishing, 1997)

Smith, J. Richard and Creek, Eddie J., *Me 262 Volumes One, Two, Three and Four* (Classic Publications, 1997–2000)

Steinhoff, Johannes, *The Last Chance – The Pilots' Plot Against Göring* (Hutchinson, 1977)

WEBSITES

B-26 Marauder Historical Society

Martin B-26 Marauder at b26.com

Library of Congress (Robert M. Ferrara Collection Interview/Recording, University of Florida Samuel Proctor Oral History Program)

National Aviation Hall of Fame

The Falcon Foundation

The Glenn L. Martin Maryland Aviation Museum

INDEX